HISTORIC
PUB CRAWLS

Through
ENGLAND

ALSO BY **THOMAS J. VOSPER**

Historic Pub Crawls Through London: Volume I
Historic Pub Crawls Through London: Volume II
Historic Pub Crawls Through New York

HISTORIC
PUB CRAWLS

Through
ENGLAND

*Eleven guided walks around England's
iconic pubs and landmarks*

THOMAS J. VOSPER

SPHERE

SPHERE

First published in Great Britain in 2023
This edition published in 2025 by Sphere

1 3 5 7 9 10 8 6 4 2

Designed by Clare Sivell
Typeset in Minion Pro by Clare Sivell
Printed and bound in Great Britain by Clays Ltd, Elcograf S.p.A

Papers used by Sphere are from well-managed forests
and other responsible sources.

Sphere	The authorised representative
An imprint of	in the EEA is
Little, Brown Book Group	Hachette Ireland
Carmelite House	8 Castlecourt Centre, Dublin 15,
50 Victoria Embankment	D15 YF6A, Ireland
London EC4Y 0DZ	(email: info@hbgi.ie)

An Hachette UK Company

www.hachette.co.uk
www.littlebrown.co.uk

To everyone that has joined me on pub crawls, and everyone still to do so.

CONTENTS

Manchester (Victoria to Piccadilly)

FOREWORD

The public house has been a cornerstone of British culture and society for centuries. In all of their glorious diversity, pubs offer us a precious third space away from home and work, where we can rub shoulders and strike up conversations with people from all social strata. In *Historic Pub Crawls Through England*, Thomas has found a way to firmly anchor our pubs within the heritage landscapes they occupy – and to encourage us all to get out of the house and explore them for ourselves.

I first met Thomas on a press trip to Amsterdam. There I was taken by his boundless enthusiasm not just for discovering great beer and wonderful establishments in which to drink it, but also his passion for sharing his discoveries with others. I could see that he was always looking for the next great shot – the juicy discovery that would delight his considerable band of online followers. It is that eye for detail, his knack for discovering the novel and unique aspects of a place, that makes this volume both eminently readable and abundantly useful as a practical guide.

In a former life, I was once a museum curator. I got to see first-hand how much the general public enjoys uncovering the fascinating stories that are locked in the historic buildings of our English cities and towns. It gives me great pleasure to read Thomas's insights into the history of the pubs that he covers because he, quite rightly, puts those narratives on an equal footing with the other venerable landmarks, buildings and sculptures that he describes in these pages.

Pubs have tangible value, rich history and cultural significance. There are few better ways to appreciate this than on foot, with friends – in a pub crawl. And what is more, our hostelries are not dead spaces. They are not tombs to a distant world that has long since crumbled. They are still living, breathing entities full of fun and joy that wait for your visit with open arms. These venues may well be able to boast a catalogue of fascinating stories from the past, but the public house is also budding with the potential for you to make your own memories there. They have a foot in the past, the present and the future. Take up Thomas's invitation, and sally forth on a historic pub crawl of your own.

Laura Hadland
Author of *50 Years of CAMRA* and *Beer Festivals: A Great British Tradition*
linktr.ee/laurahadland

ABOUT THIS BOOK

Having spent the last sixteen years arranging pub crawls with my friends and family, this book is a tribute to the locations and pubs that I have personally visited.

While every effort has been made to ensure its accuracy at the time of going to print, there may be subsequent name changes or, worse, a pub may have ceased trading.

There are always more pubs to visit and, while I try to share the most interesting places (with the best beer), each crawl is planned more for the enjoyment of an entire route, prioritising an interesting area over any individual pub.

I have not made any commercial agreements to endorse any pubs, and sadly we miss out, or walk past, great pubs all the time – usually just to ensure we space out the route to sufficiently sober up between stops.

This book has no rules and is merely a guide for you to explore an area and the pubs within. If you pass a pub that looks good, pop in – you never know what you might find!

PREFACE

There are more than 38,000 pubs across England and, after the release of my first book of pub crawls exploring some of the 3,500 in the capital, I spent the subsequent six months revisiting more than 250 of them to film them for social media. This number is a drop in the ocean when you consider the pubs, inns and taverns that are the backbone of towns and cities across our nation.

Wherever you are on this island, there is always a pub nearby – on a busy road, down a country lane or as the last hold-out of a centuries-old building hemmed in by new developments.

Over sixteen years I have honed my talent when it comes to pub crawl arranging (a very valuable skill, if you ask me).

What started as a birthday treat enjoyed by family and friends has become a deeper passion, and a way to explore cities and towns across England and beyond.

I started in London, my home town, writing about well-trodden routes I knew like the back of my hand. As my social media following grew, I became emboldened by my new followers' enthusiasm to explore further afield, and to cover pubs that were important to people across the country.

When you arrive in a new town or city, the pub is often the best place to start, maybe stop off for lunch, or end a day's exploring.

The pubs and their regulars always have amazing stories to tell, and a good team behind the bar will make a stranger feel at home.

I won't share much in the way of long descriptions or opinions of pubs in this book, nor will I recount all of the stories I've been told. I have learned from the success of my first few books that I am merely a guide in your journey. You, dear crawler, must have the freedom to discover your own path.

The complete routes are typically around a couple of miles, with a total walk time of around an hour and the gap between pubs often being five to ten minutes, allowing for sufficient fresh air and recovery to maintain the energy and thirst for the next pint.

Many hours have been spent laughing over a beer with friends, so I am honoured to explore our amazing country and share these fascinating pubs, showcasing some of the most iconic locations across our amazing towns and cities.

Hopefully you will enjoy these routes and get to discover the stories behind the pubs for yourself as we do our bit to support the pubs and their rich heritage.

The best times in life are those spent with family and friends, and if you're on one of my pub crawls that's exactly what you are.

HOW TO USE THIS GUIDE

Each route starts near a train station or landmark, with walking directions and a map.

Throughout the directions, areas of interest, landmarks or facts are marked with letters corresponding to details in the pages that follow.

This book is designed to fit in your back pocket and be easy to carry as you explore the routes.

Should you wish to skip any pubs, or find your own route, full pub details are provided for you to plot your own path.

Often the routes have a few pubs condensed into a short distance, enabling you to curate your own shorter path.

Timings are provided as a guide, to ensure you can complete the route with an early afternoon start time.

HISTORIC
PUB CRAWLS

Through
ENGLAND

ST ALBANS
(The Cock to the Horn)

Famous for – at one point – hosting the most pubs per square mile in the UK, this cathedral city offers a very varied range of pubs and places to stop to eat.

This station-to-station route starts by the Roman park and heads past the spectacular cathedral before winding through the town centre and back streets.

It is a mix of historic pubs (including what is rumoured to be the country's oldest) along with more modern music venues and CAMRA (Campaign for Real Ale) award winners.

This route is perfect for absorbing the atmosphere of an ancient market town that was the lynchpin of the Roman occupation of England.

Start from St Albans Abbey station (AL1 2AY).

1. **Ye Olde Fighting Cocks** *1.30 p.m.*
16 Abbey Mill Lane, AL3 4HE

2. **Mad Squirrel (closed Monday)** *2.30 p.m.*
Heritage Close, 17 High Street, AL3 4EB

3. **The Boot** *3.00 p.m.*
4 Market Place, AL3 5DG

4. **The Peahen** *3.45 p.m.*
14 London Road, AL1 1NG

5. **The White Hart** *4.30 p.m.*
23–25 Holywell Hill, AL1 1EZ

6. **The Garibaldi** *5.15 p.m.*
61 Albert Street, AL1 1RT

7. **The Beehive** *5.45 p.m.*
2 Keyfield Terrace, AL1 1QL

8. **The Farmer's Boy** *6.15 p.m.*
134 London Road, AL1 1PQ

9. **The Victoria** *6.45 p.m.*
82 Victoria Street, AL1 3TG

10. **Robin Hood** *7.30 p.m.*
126 Victoria Street, AL1 3TG

11. **The Horn** *8.15 p.m.*
Victoria Street, AL1 3TE

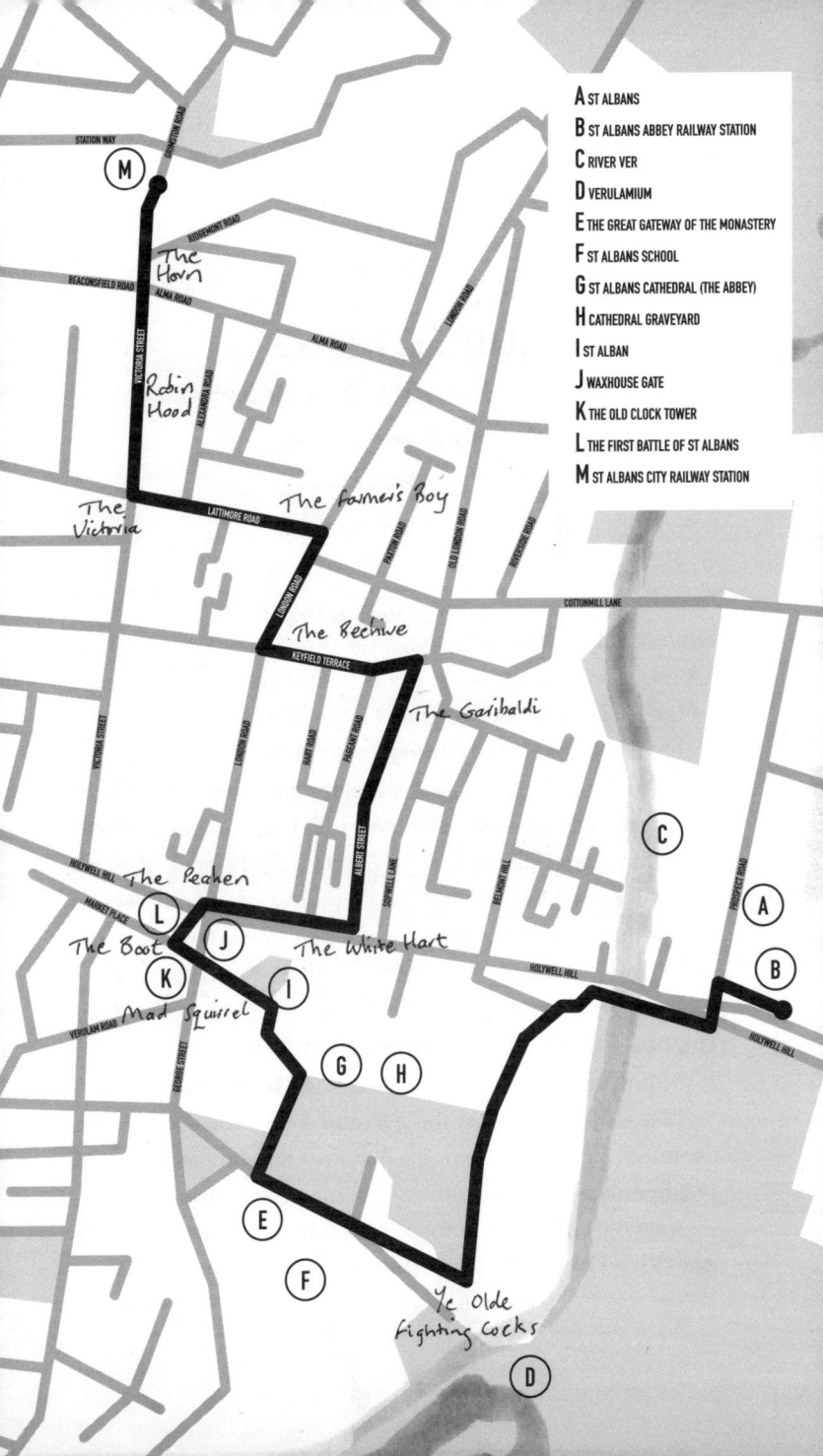

A ST ALBANS
B ST ALBANS ABBEY RAILWAY STATION
C RIVER VER
D VERULAMIUM
E THE GREAT GATEWAY OF THE MONASTERY
F ST ALBANS SCHOOL
G ST ALBANS CATHEDRAL (THE ABBEY)
H CATHEDRAL GRAVEYARD
I ST ALBAN
J WAXHOUSE GATE
K THE OLD CLOCK TOWER
L THE FIRST BATTLE OF ST ALBANS
M ST ALBANS CITY RAILWAY STATION

DIRECTIONS

Leave the station **(A, B)** through the car park and take the first left after crossing the River Ver **(C)**. Take the public footpath on the left, which leads to an open space, and follow the edge of the field to **Ye Olde Fighting Cocks (1, D)**.

Leave the pub and head up the slope of Abbey Mill Lane to the Great Gateway of the Monastery **(E, F)** before turning and following alongside the Abbey **(G, H)** on the right. At the end of the Abbey **(I)**, turn left up the alleyway to **Mad Squirrel (2)**.

Continue along the passage, though Waxhouse Gate **(J)**, where the Old Clock Tower **(K)** is opposite **The Boot (3, L)**.

Turn left from the pub, and left at the main road, where **The Peahen (4)** sits on the first corner, before turning right at the pub and heading down the hill to **The White Hart (5)**.

Take the first left past the pub and follow the road to **The Garibaldi (6)** before turning left at the end of the road where **The Beehive (7)** is along an alley at the dead end.

Turn right at the main road and follow it until **The Farmer's Boy (8)**, on the same side of the road.

Exit the pub and cross to Lattimore Road, where at the end, on the corner, is **The Victoria (9)**.

Turn right out of the pub, where **Robin Hood (10)** is on the right, with **The Horn (11)** further along the road **(M)**.

A. ST ALBANS

Located in the south of England, not far from London, St Albans is a beautiful cathedral city with a lot of history. There has been a settlement here since the Iron Age, and it was already a major centre of trade and power before the Romans invaded in AD 43. A large portion of the ancient city remains and can be seen by visitors to the central park.

After the Roman withdrawal in 410 the town fell under control of the Anglo-Saxon tribe the Waeclingas, who, along with the Brahhingas and Hicce, were one of the most important tribes throughout Hertfordshire.

By 1077, St Albans Abbey had become the principal medieval abbey in England.

The twice-weekly street market was originally founded by the Abbot Ulsinus in 948, meaning all the vendors had to be Church approved and the abbot had the ultimate say in all matters regarding the market. In 1553, Edward VI sold the rights to the town itself, loosening some of the rules on who could run a stall and what could be traded.

Its location as the last stop on the route to London from the north meant many travellers would rest their weary heads in the city. This supported many old coaching inns and taverns.

The railway arrived in 1858, and in the late nineteenth century the population expanded rapidly, rising by 37 per cent between 1891 and 1901.

St Albans was granted city status and the abbey was granted cathedral status in 1877 by Queen Victoria's royal charter.

B. ST ALBANS ABBEY RAILWAY STATION

In 2009 this small, open-air station at the end of the line was just the second station in the country to accommodate the installation of a Harrington Hump – the partially raised section of the platform that ensures easier access for wheelchair users, pushchairs and others with mobility issues. The feature is named after Harrington station in Cumbria, England, which was the location of the first installation.

It was the first station built in St Albans, in 1858; although the much busier City station opened ten years later, it was not until 1924 that 'Abbey' was added to this station's name.

C. RIVER VER

This chalk stream acts as a tributary (a small river that joins a larger one) to the River Colne and runs for 17 miles from its source in nearby Kensworth Lynch.

It used to be a notable landmark used in navigation, which led to many Roman constructions along its banks – this trend to build in valleys was counter to the common approach of building at high points. Native Britons tended to build on higher ground, to be able to see for a further distance. Romans preferred to stay low and hidden.

Going over the River Ver on St Michael's Street is the oldest arched bridge in Hertfordshire, which dates from 1765. It is believed that a bridge was built here around AD 200, and the adjacent ford, which has been there for two millennia, is thought to be where St Alban himself crossed the river on the way to his execution.

D. VERULAMIUM

St Albans was the first major Roman town north of what is now London and was at the time called Verulamium – it was one of the largest settlements in Roman Britain behind Londinium.

The city is also famous because of the historic Watling Street, which starts in Dover before passing over the Thames in London, and leads all the way to Wales via St Albans. Although it had been used by Ancient Britons, it was one of the major Roman routes and they went to great effort to pave the length of it.

Despite agriculture damaging much of the remains, research has been able to identify outlines of buildings and the town's layout following the Roman settlement. It has changed much over time, but the Verulamium Museum has maps and models to help visitors imagine how the town would have looked all those years (and a name change) ago.

The population grew, and the town was ransacked by Boudica and her Iceni tribe in AD 61, but it recovered and despite two significant fires, in 155 and 250, it was rebuilt in stone and included a forum, basilica and theatre – the remains can still be seen today.

Unfortunately, much of the original Roman settlement was quarried for building materials to create the Norman abbey.

Verulamium

1. YE OLDE FIGHTING COCKS

While it has historically been described as the oldest pub in England, the title was withdrawn in 2000 as it was deemed impossible to verify. The owners claim that the pub has been open since 793, although the source of that information is somewhat shaky.

The earliest mentioned licences are in 1756, but the building appears to be from the sixteenth century and its distinctive octagonal shape means it is widely believed the building used to be a pigeon house – once lending it the name the Three Pigeons. This name was abandoned some time ago, with another bird taking over the mantle. The current name is believed to come from the 'sport' of cockfighting which probably took place under the low ceilings in this grade II listed building.

Over time, there have been many additions to the structure. Notably, in 1539, the whole building was moved to the current location from a site closer to the cathedral. There is a long-standing rumour that there used to be tunnels from the cellars to the cathedral, but if this is true they have been filled in. Although it is unclear what was on the site before 1539, the foundations have been dated to around 793.

E. THE GREAT GATEWAY OF THE MONASTERY

Built in 1365, this imposing building is the last remnant of the Benedictine monastery (other than the Abbey itself) and has been part of the adjacent school since 1871.

It was besieged in 1381 during the Peasants' Revolt, and has been used as a prison (in 1539) and home to a printing press (1479).

F. ST ALBANS SCHOOL

Founded in 948 by a local abbot – Wulsin – it is the only English-speaking school to have educated a pope. Born Nicholas Breakspear in Hertfordshire around 1100, Pope Adrian IV was pope from 1154–1159 and is (so far) the only English pope.

As well as Pope Adrian IV, other famous alumni include physicist Ian Grant, archaeologist Colin Renfrew and Stringfellows fan and iconic scientist Stephen Hawking.

The school's motto is *non nobis nati* ('Born not for ourselves') and it has often been labelled as one of the oldest in the world.

G. ST ALBANS CATHEDRAL (THE ABBEY)

Only officially becoming a cathedral in 1877, the abbey was most likely founded around the eighth century before losing its abbey status in the sixteenth century after Henry VIII's dissolution of the monasteries.

Its 280-foot nave is notable as the country's longest, and the construction includes Norman and Romanesque architecture of the eleventh century along with later Gothic and nineteenth-century additions.

There is very limited information on the first iterations of the abbey, but we know King Offa II of Mercia founded a monastery in 793. Around a hundred years later it was probably sacked by Danish raiders, forcing the reigning Abbot Ealdred to start removing building material from the remains of Verulamium – although continuous raids stalled their efforts to rebuild the structure.

In total, there are twenty-three bells housed in the tower, with the oldest cast around 1290 and still used as the sanctus bell. This type of bell is rung during services to highlight important moments.

The impressive presence of St Albans Cathedral dominates the area.

H. CATHEDRAL GRAVEYARD

The burial grounds are the final resting place of a few famous historical figures, including Robert Breakspear, the father of the aforementioned English Pope, Adrian IV. He died in 1110, when his son was around ten years old.

Later, in 1370, Adam Rous was laid to rest here. Rous spent his life as the royal surgeon to King Henry III.

The royal connections do not end there, as the fourth son of King Henry IV, Humphrey Duke of Gloucester, was buried here in 1447. Humphrey was a controversial figure in his time, advising for his brother, King Henry V, and nephew, King Henry VI.

Bringing us into a more modern time, Robert Runcie was buried here in 2000. He was at one point the Bishop of St Albans, but was promoted to Archbishop of Canterbury, making him the leader of the Church of England between 1980 and 1991.

I. ST ALBAN

Saint Alban was Britain's first Christian martyr saint; he lived in Verulamium during the third or fourth centuries, a time of extreme Christian persecution.

Legend has it that, after providing safe haven for a priest, he converted to Christianity. Later, when Roman soldiers raided the property, he sacrificed himself by claiming to be the priest.

As the fatal blow in his beheading was delivered, it was said that the executioner's eyes popped out and fell beside Alban's decapitated head. The eyes and the head then all rolled down the hill to a site where a natural well suddenly sprang up.

2. MAD SQUIRREL

This modern taproom is linked to the brewery of the same name which was established in 2010. The venue is famous for its beer garden, which overlooks the cathedral.

J. WAXHOUSE GATE

Surviving now as an open passageway, this alley provides access from the town to the north of the abbey.

Although eighteenth century in style, this appearance is derived from restoration work. It is believed to have been constructed as early as 1427 by Abbot John of Wheathampstead.

Emerging from the alley straight into the market square.

K. THE OLD CLOCK TOWER

This grade I listed building was constructed between 1403 and 1412 and lays claim to being the only surviving medieval town belfry in England. It stands near the site of a now-demolished Eleanor cross, which was built to mark where the funeral procession for Edward I's wife stopped overnight in 1290.

Believed to have been constructed as a protest against the local abbey's attempts to regulate timekeeping in the town, the tower contained a shop, a home for the owner and living quarters for the clock keepers.

Although the exact date of the clock's installation is unknown, the building of this type of structure was a rare occurrence around this time. The two bells (Gabriel and the Market Bell) span several centuries. The former was cast around 1335 and rang at 4 a.m., to mark the Angelus, before ringing again to mark curfew at around 8 p.m.

The Market Bell was installed much later, around 1729, to notify residents and traders of the opening of the market for those who were not freemen of the town – originally only freemen were allowed to trade before 10 a.m. The bell remained in operation for this purpose until 1835.

3. THE BOOT

This grade II listed building dates to 1500 and has been known as the Old Wellington and the Blue Boar.

While its current name is rumoured to come from a thirteenth-century priest who trapped the devil in a boot he placed outside the pub, the more likely explanation is linked to the various tanners and leather market nearby.

L. THE FIRST BATTLE OF ST ALBANS

Taking place in 1455, the First Battle of St Albans is generally accepted as being the beginning of the Wars of the Roses between Richard, Duke of York, and Henry VI.

Usually, battles took place in a large, expansive area, but in

St Albans the fighting took place within the confines of the town: on the streets and within the taverns.

The aftermath of this battle was a complete victory for York and resulted in the capture of the King, Henry VI.

The wars ended in 1487, with Henry Tudor (son of Henry VI and later Henry VII) killing Richard. Henry then married Elizabeth of York, uniting the two warring factions. Their son, King Henry VIII, had claims on both sides to the throne.

4. THE PEAHEN

Although merged with the adjoining Woolpack pub in the eighteenth century, the Peahen is first mentioned as far back as 1480.

As one of the trading hotels on the London Road, it became a vital stopping point on journeys to and from the capital before the original building burned down around the end of the nineteenth century.

Since 1938 it has been under the ownership of McMullen & Sons, Hertfordshire-based brewers who have been operating since 1827.

On my last visit we met a group of lads who taught us a drinking game with gin, where we all drank a shot – one was gin and the rest were water – and we had to guess who had the gin. On the third and final round, unknown to all of us, every shot was gin.

5. THE WHITE HART

Another contender for the oldest pub in England, the hotel dates to 1470 and was one of the original coaching inns along the London Road.

It is rumoured to be haunted by several ghosts, notably a lady who broke her neck on the low entrance when she failed to duck while sitting in the high cheap seats of a carriage, and a twelve-year-old girl, who is often spotted on the back steps. It is believed she died in an 1832 fire.

It is known as the final stop of Simon Fraser, the 11th Lord Lovat, who passed by on his way to become the final person in Britain to be beheaded, after being charged with high treason. He was beheaded in April 1747, and the event was so crowded a stand collapsed, killing several people.

6. THE GARIBALDI

This back-street pub was named after the nineteenth-century Italian exile, who was believed to have lived in St Albans for a period.

A popular figure in his day, Giuseppe Garibaldi is best known as a military figure and revolutionary who is considered to be one of the 'fathers' of modern Italy.

He is also honoured by the creation of the Garibaldi biscuit, which is two thin, doughy biscuits separated by a layer of crushed currants. First manufactured in London in 1861, their appearance has earned them the nicknames fly sandwiches, flies' graveyards and dead-fly biscuits.

7. THE BEEHIVE

This double-bay-window fronted building has a large beer garden and is a popular sports pub in the area.

One of the joys of life: sitting in a beer garden when the sun is shining.

8. THE FARMER'S BOY

This cottage-style pub is well known for showcasing live music and hosting craft-beer festivals in its garden.

9. THE VICTORIA

Now operating as a sports bar, this pub has had many guises and names, including the Acorn, Clannard and Glass House.

Although pretty generic in style, considering the variety of pubs in the area, this is a laid-back, stripped-down bar that is perfect for catching live sport on the big screen.

10. ROBIN HOOD

A regular CAMRA award winner, this pub is known both for its craft ales and cider as well as a varied selection of pickled eggs behind the bar.

I loved this pub because of the eggs, and every time I return there is a different one to try.

Famous for its cider and pickled eggs, with a selection of the latter behind the bar that I couldn't wait to get stuck into.

11. THE HORN

Originally a hotel, this pub is linked to the nearby station and the Midland Railway hotel opposite. Starting in the 1960s with occasional performances, it worked its way into becoming a famed music venue known as the Horn of Plenty in the 1970s.

As well as formerly being run by footballer and Hollywood actor Vinnie Jones's mum, it has started the careers of many household names. Famous acts who have performed here include Paul Young, Bad Manners, the Bluetones, Toploader, Tom Grennan, U2 and Turin Brakes.

Radio presenter John Peel was a notable former patron, and singer Kim Wilde used to work behind the bar.

My favourite memory of the Horn was recording a spoof tribute to one of my favourite comedy magic acts, 'Siegfried & Joy', as we roped a couple of the locals into the trick of my vanishing outside the front door before re-emerging (pint in hand at the bar). A few months later I would join them on-stage during their European tour.

M. ST ALBANS CITY RAILWAY STATION

The larger of the two stations, it was built by Midland Railway in 1868 on the main line into London St Pancras.

At the time, St Albans was a notable producer of watercress, which was sent from here to London and Manchester on the train.

BRIGHTON
(Station to Seaside)

Whether it is the winding, narrow and somewhat eccentric streets or the spectacular pier and seafront, there is always something to see in Brighton.

It was mentioned in the Domesday Book of 1086 as 'Brighthelmstone' and since the Georgian era it has been a popular and fashionable seaside resort. People would flock from London to the coast, and rail improvements opened up the trip to a wider variety of people than ever before.

Starting at the station, the route winds down the hill and through the iconic Lanes before ending at the seafront for a well-earned bag of fish and chips overlooking the shingle beach. Just look out for any seagulls that might fancy a bite of your lunch.

Brighton is one of my favourite towns and, although it can sometimes feel incredibly busy, the eclectic mix of people and places – especially in the Lanes – is delightful. As well as its historic buildings, Brighton is famous for its diverse culture and inclusiveness, so a pub crawl here is sure to be eclectic.

Start from Brighton station (BN1 3XP).

1. **The Queen's Head** *1.00 p.m.*
69 Queens Road, BN1 3XD

2. **The Grand Central** *1.30 p.m.*
29–30 Surrey Street, BN1 3PA

3. **The Prince Albert** *2.00 p.m.*
48 Trafalgar Street, BN1 4ED

4. **The Green Dragon** *2.45 p.m.*
8–9 Sydney Street, BN1 4EN

5. **Ye Olde King & Queen** *3.15 p.m.*
13–17 Marlborough Place, BN1 1UB

6. **The Mucky Duck** *4.00 p.m.*
7–9 Manchester Street, BN2 1TF

7. **The Pump House** *4.45 p.m.*
46 Market Street, BN1 1HH

East Street Tap
74 East Street, BN1 1HQ

8. **The Cricketers** *5.30 p.m.*
15 Black Lion Street, BN1 1ND

9. **The Black Lion** *6.00 p.m.*
14 Black Lion Street, BN1 1ND

10. **Seven Stars** *6.30 p.m.*
27 Ship Street, BN1 1AD

11. **Victory** *7.15 p.m.*
6 Duke Street, BN1 1AH

12. **Fortune of War** *8.00 p.m.*
156 Kings Road, BN1 1NB

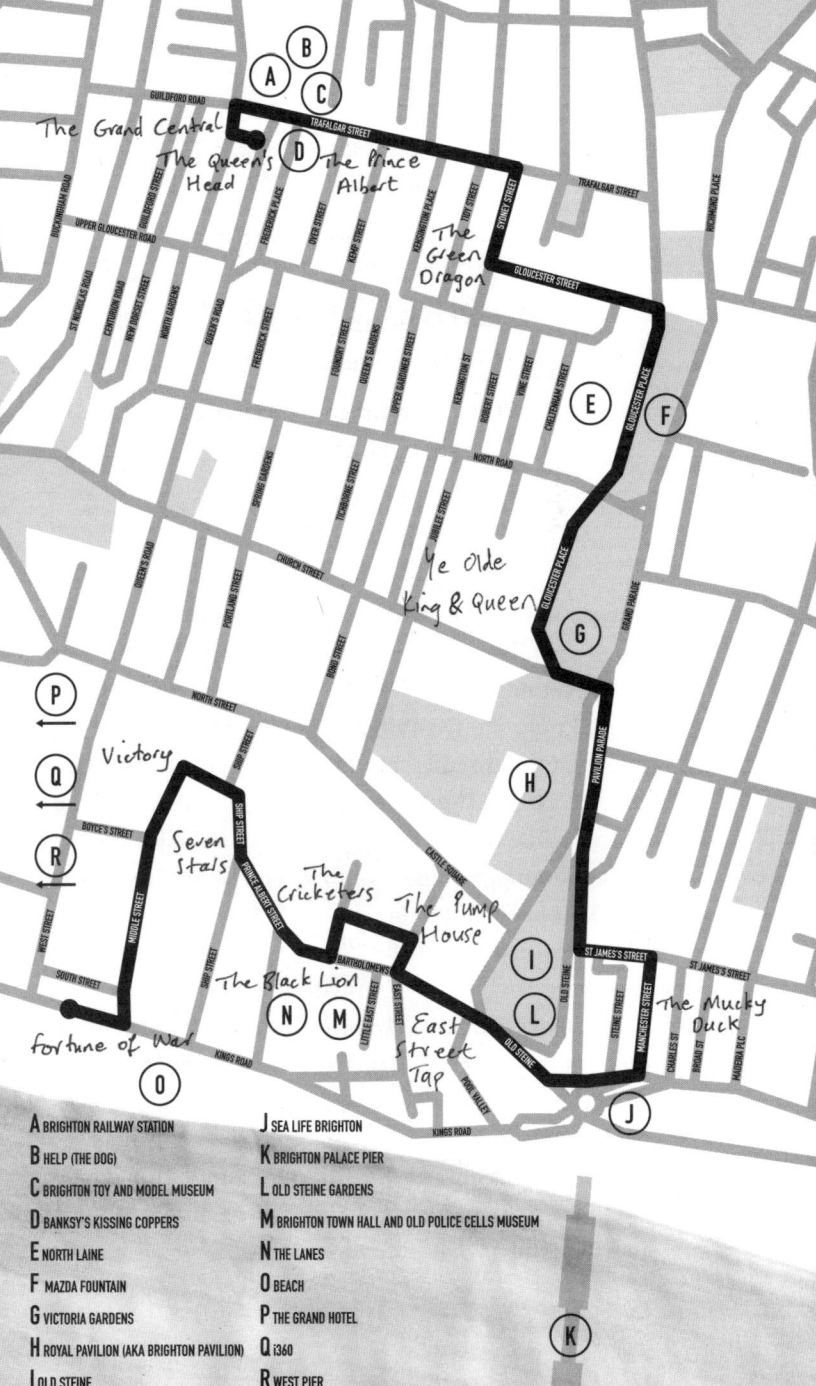

The Grand Central
The Queen's Head
The Prince Albert
The Green Dragon
Ye Olde King & Queen
Victory
Seven Stars
The Cricketers
The Pump House
The Black Lion
East Street Tap
fortune of War
The Mucky Duck

Ⓐ Ⓑ Ⓒ Ⓓ Ⓔ Ⓕ Ⓖ Ⓗ Ⓘ Ⓙ Ⓚ Ⓛ Ⓜ Ⓝ Ⓞ Ⓟ Ⓠ Ⓡ

A BRIGHTON RAILWAY STATION
B HELP (THE DOG)
C BRIGHTON TOY AND MODEL MUSEUM
D BANKSY'S KISSING COPPERS
E NORTH LAINE
F MAZDA FOUNTAIN
G VICTORIA GARDENS
H ROYAL PAVILION (AKA BRIGHTON PAVILION)
I OLD STEINE
J SEA LIFE BRIGHTON
K BRIGHTON PALACE PIER
L OLD STEINE GARDENS
M BRIGHTON TOWN HALL AND OLD POLICE CELLS MUSEUM
N THE LANES
O BEACH
P THE GRAND HOTEL
Q i360
R WEST PIER

DIRECTIONS

Exit the station **(A, B)** and head to **The Queen's Head (1)** at the top of the hill. Exit the pub left, back towards the station, where **The Grand Central (2)** is to its left. Head down the underpass **(C)** opposite **The Prince Albert (3, D)**.

Follow the road right from the pub and turn right along Sydney Street **(E)** to **The Green Dragon (4)**. Leave the pub and take the opposite road before turning right at Valley Gardens **(F)** and continuing alongside until you reach **Ye Olde King & Queen (5)** opposite Victoria Gardens **(G)**.

Follow the gardens as the road curves left, to head towards the sea along Pavilion Parade, with the Royal Pavilion and then Old Steine Gardens **(H, I)** to your right, before turning left on St James's Street where **The Mucky Duck (6)** is along the second right.

Exit the pub right, and turn right on the main road, opposite Sea Life Brighton **(J, K)**. Turn right at the roundabout, following the road to the left of Old Steine Gardens **(L)**. Take the narrow road that is second left and follow Pool Valley

Passage as it bends left then right, before emerging at an optional pub, **East Street Tap (7)**, on the corner. Exit the pub to the right and follow the road as it curves left before taking the right after the Town Hall **(M)** to **The Pump House (7)**. After retracing to the main road, turn right towards **The Cricketers (8)** which is at the heart of the Lanes **(N)** and next to **The Black Lion (9)**.

Turn left from the pub, and follow the road left, before heading right as it merges with Ship Street, and the **Seven Stars (10)** is on the opposite side of the road. Continue left, past the pub to the **Victory (11)** on the corner, before heading left towards the sea, where the **Fortune of War (12)** is under the arches, directly on the beach **(O)** before the Grand Hotel **(P)**, under the watchful gaze of the i360 **(Q)** and overlooking the derelict West Pier **(R)**.

A. BRIGHTON RAILWAY STATION

The seventh biggest station in the UK outside London, it was built between 1840 and 1846 by the London and Brighton Railway Company.

The distinctive three-storey building originally housed the railway company's headquarters and is built in an Italianate style. It was designed by renowned architect David Mocatta, who also designed synagogues during his lifetime.

These days the original building is partly hidden by a gabled canopy that was designed and constructed in 1882–83.

Underneath the station, the goods yards were repurposed into offices during World War II – with a section of tunnels still used as a shooting range by a local rifle club.

The roof at Brighton station is an impressive welcome.

B. HELP (THE DOG)

Before Toto, Lassie or Scooby-Doo, Help the dog was a famous pooch. At the time of his death in 1891, the thirteen-year-old Scotch collie was probably the best-known dog in the UK.

A railway guard, John Climpson, had the idea of using a dog to collect money for the Railway Servants' Orphan Fund, and Help was supplied with a specially fitted wooden box on his back that was inscribed with the words 'I am Help, the railway dog of England, and travelling agent for the orphans of railwaymen who are killed on duty.'

He didn't always travel with his owner, and took collections on other routes across national lines, most major towns and even two trips to France. He managed to raise more than £1,000 during his lifetime – which is the equivalent of about £159,000 today.

Following his death, he was stuffed and displayed in the station, with his efforts inspiring others such as Prince (in

Croydon), Nell (in Bournemouth), Tim (in Paddington) and Basingstoke Jack (no points for guessing where that one lived).

1. THE QUEEN'S HEAD

Queen's Road was constructed in 1845 to improve access between the city centre and the new railway station. It was so successful and well used that, by 1878, the road needed widening to accommodate all the traffic.

While the pub did not originally face the station, the demolition of two buildings in the effort to widen the road exposed this three-storey building and led to the installation of a façade typical for that time.

2. THE GRAND CENTRAL

Originally a hotel, the Grand Central was built in 1840 to service passengers from the new mainline station.

As trade dwindled, it converted to a pub in 1925, with the upstairs now including a gin bar, theatre and secret roof garden.

C. BRIGHTON TOY AND MODEL MUSEUM

Nestled under the Victorian arches that support the railway station, and occupying over 4,000 square feet of floor space, this museum was opened in 1991 and showcases more than 10,000 toys and models.

Alongside toys from the likes of Dinky, Corgi, Hornby, Meccano and Bing, it often features guest collections.

When the railway arches were built in 1841, they were primarily used as storage for a local brewery, with up to four dray horses living in what is now the museum entrance.

It was acquired and renovated by a charitable trust founded by Christopher Littledale, who remains the museum's director.

3. THE PRINCE ALBERT

Originally a three-storey townhouse that was built in 1848, this striking building was converted into a pub in 1860.

The location of Banksy's famous *Kissing Coppers* art installation, the mural was extended in 2013 when local graffiti artists Req and Sinna One depicted twenty-six deceased musicians, as well as actor Oliver Reed and footballer George Best, on the wall, with a multicoloured backdrop. An additional twenty-four deceased musicians were added in 2017.

The artwork continues through the pub, which is notable for hosting live music performances almost every night of the year.

Tobias, of 'weeklyhistory', found an amusing spot in the beer garden.

D. BANKSY'S KISSING COPPERS

Often regarded as one of street artist Banksy's most notable works, this mural appeared on the side of the Prince Albert pub in 2004.

The black and white painting shows two male police officers, in full uniform, locked in an embrace. Its location is thought to be significant, given Brighton's reputation as the LGBTQ+ capital of the UK.

Due to the speed required when erecting the images, to maintain the artist's anonymity, it is a great example of stencil graffiti – which allows the artist to quickly and accurately apply layers of paint over a cut-out design.

The pub landlord caused controversy in 2008 by replacing the original with a replica due to repeated vandalism, and he later sold the artwork, in 2014, for $575,000 to an anonymous buyer at a Miami auction.

E. NORTH LAINE

Once considered the slum area of the city, its rabble of cafés, pubs, theatres and museums is now seen as Brighton's cultural quarter.

Since the Middle Ages the surrounding area has been occupied by five 'Laines' – an Anglo-Saxon term for open farming plots.

As the expansion of Brighton in the nineteenth century started to encroach on the fields, the boundary lines were converted into streets and the area began to develop a market and railway hub.

4. THE GREEN DRAGON

This otherwise unremarkable single bar hides an intimate beer garden that can be found by following the dragon footprints through the pub.

Formerly called the Office, it is notable for its eclectic interior, distinctive ceiling and decorated beer garden.

I was joined to film this for my social media accounts by my friend Tobias, who runs 'weeklyhistory' and is local to the area.

F. MAZDA FOUNTAIN

Gifted to the city by Thomson-Houston Ltd in 1930, many consider this fountain to be symbolic of Brighton. The original technology used to light the distinctive design became obsolete and dysfunctional, and for more than thirty years the fountain remained unlit. In 2015 it was drained, and the council said there was no budget to repair it, but a petition was started that ultimately led to the restoration and modernisation of the Mazda Fountain four years later. Nowadays, easy to maintain LEDs will light the fountain for years to come.

5. YE OLDE KING & QUEEN

Named in honour of George III and Charlotte, this mock-Tudor pub is on the site of a former farmhouse that was constructed in 1779 and is believed to have been turned into a pub around 1860.

At the time, the town had approximately one pub for every thirty households, so each had to try to stand out. This building served various functions such as the local corn exchange, a riding school, a barracks and a courthouse, as well as more traditional pub roles.

The pub and most of the adjoining buildings were rebuilt in the 1930s, with the interior including stained-glass panels and a barrel-vaulted wooden ceiling at first-floor level.

The three main ground-floor rooms were amalgamated to form a spacious medieval nobleman's hall, which has hosted a variety of events, from the Conservative Party Conference's overspill through to the regular 'Miss Miniskirt' pageant.

G. VICTORIA GARDENS

One of the most popular public parks in the area, its name pays tribute to Queen Victoria. She is honoured with a statue, by sculptor Carlo Nicoli, that was presented by Sir John George Blaker in 1897 to commemorate the queen's diamond jubilee.

Once a barren, flat space that formed a central area in the city, over time the park has evolved to become home to flower beds and trees.

H. ROYAL PAVILION (AKA BRIGHTON PAVILION)

This former royal residence was constructed between 1787 and 1823. Its Indo-Saracenic style was prevalent through India for most of the nineteenth century, and it features domes and minarets designed by one of Britain's foremost architects, John Nash – who is best known for another royal residence: Buckingham Palace.

Before ascending to the throne as George IV, the then Prince of Wales first visited Brighton at the age of twenty-one. He was said to have enjoyed the area, leading to an increase in the fame and popularity of the town. The pavilion was planned and built for the future king to escape the financial investigations relating to the building of his London residence, Carlton House, and as a place to liaise with his long-time companion, Maria Fitzherbert.

Initially the prince commissioned Henry Holland, who had designed Carlton House, to enlarge an existing building at the edge of the Old Steine.

This first construction became one wing of the Marine Pavilion, flanking a central rotunda, and contained three opulent rooms fitted out in Holland's French-influenced neoclassical style.

By 1802, the pavilion had been enlarged to include a new dining room and conservatory. Following the purchase of the surrounding land, a riding school and stables were added in an Indian style to provide stabling for sixty horses. The final work was undertaken by John Nash and occurred between 1815 and 1822, primarily greatly extending the pavilion.

During World War I, the buildings were converted into a military hospital, where many wounded soldiers from the Indian Army, including recipients of the Victoria Cross, were cared for. At its peak it housed 720 beds and treated more than 2,300 soldiers. A new gateway opened in 1921 to commemorate its wartime role.

After being purchased by a charitable trust, its move from private to public building meant it became a popular tourist destination, with around 400,000 annual visitors.

The Royal Pavilion

I. OLD STEINE

Originally a stream running adjacent to the easternmost dwellings of Brighthelmstone, the area was used by local fishermen to lay out and dry their nets.

The word 'Steine' derives from the Old English 'stoene', meaning 'stony place', and the name is thought to refer to the sarsen stones that once lay in the area – examples of which can be seen at the base of the Victoria Fountain, which was built in 1823.

6. THE MUCKY DUCK

Opened as the Star Inn in 1865, this tiled-fronted pub is notable for its US-president themed urinals. Sorry, ladies, I didn't risk seeing if there was anything interesting in your loos.

J. SEA LIFE BRIGHTON

Opened in 1872, it is the oldest continually operating aquarium in the world and, at the time of opening, held the largest tank in the world.

The scheme to construct the aquarium was inspired by Hyde Park's Great Exhibition in 1851 and the increasing popularity of the aquatic exhibits in the Crystal Palace.

Prolific pleasure pier designer and engineer Eugenius Birch, who was responsible for building Brighton's West Pier in 1866, conceived the design in the 1850s, with work commencing in 1869.

The area required significant work to prepare for development, including widening roads, reclaiming land from the sea and creating a new seafront road. The final cost of the building was £130,000 and the aquarium was opened by Prince Arthur, Queen Victoria's seventh child, on Easter Monday. However, the building was actually largely unfinished at the time, so a more formal opening ceremony took place during the summer of the same year.

K. BRIGHTON PALACE PIER (AKA BRIGHTON PIER, PALACE PIER)

The third pier to be constructed in Brighton, it was opened in 1899 and is the only one still in operation.

It was originally intended to replace the Royal Suspension Chain Pier, which collapsed in 1896. The new pier quickly became a popular destination for theatre and music lovers.

The iconic landmark saw early career performances from both Stan Laurel and Charlie Chaplin before they moved and found major commercial success in Hollywood.

After the theatre was damaged it was demolished in 1986 to make way for an amusement park featuring fairground rides and rollercoasters.

L. OLD STEINE GARDENS

A one-way road system introduced in 1926 encircles this triangular section of land that was once considered part of the lawns of the Royal Pavilion and houses several monuments.

It contains the impressive Victoria Fountain, which stands at 32 feet tall and features a large cast iron pool that would have originally contained water lilies and fish.

Despite the town commissioners declining the installation,

it was funded by public subscription and financed by local politician Sir John Cordy Burrows.

The fountain was inaugurated in May 1846 to celebrate the twenty-seventh birthday of Queen Victoria, and a royal salute was fired from the nearby pier.

The gardens also contain a statue of Sir John Cordy Burrows, a prominent doctor as well as a politician. Burrows was born in Ipswich, before joining the Royal College of Surgeons in 1836 and opening his practice in Brighton.

Alongside his professional practice, he was notable for his contributions to the Linnean, Zoological and Geographical societies, and he was brigade surgeon to the artillery corps and chairman of the lifeboat committee.

The Brighton War Memorial features a large, shallow pool with a central fountain and a U-shaped colonnade of stone pillars which was unveiled by Admiral David Richard Beatty in 1922.

In the far northern tip of the park stands a polished granite obelisk that commemorates the Egyptian Campaign of 1882 – which resulted in the British conquest of Egypt – and the Nile Expedition – as the British withdrew from Sudan – in 1884–85.

Wherever the route takes you, it always leads to one place.

7. EAST STREET TAP

Believed to be one of Brighton's oldest pubs, dating back to 1568, it was previously known as the Fishbowl and has since become renowned as a music venue.

On a visit to Brighton I ended up here late into the night with my friend Joey Evans, who is better known as his rock musician alter ego Evawolf.

My good friend Joey, who is better known as rock musician Evawolf, joined me at the East Street Tap.

M. BRIGHTON TOWN HALL AND OLD POLICE CELLS MUSEUM

Built in 1832, the grade II listed building is the former offices of Brighton Borough Council.

There has been a building on the site since 1514, when it was occupied by monks and their home, the Priory of Bartholomew. After it disappeared the site was used as a marketplace during the seventeenth century before the current building was commissioned.

Construction started in 1830, with the design in the Greek

revival style and the building opening two years later at a cost of £60,000.

In 1858, author Charles Dickens delivered a reading of *A Christmas Carol* to a large audience.

In the 1960s, several police holding cells were added to house the accused just before they were taken to trial in the council buildings. They fell into disrepair, but several were restored and opened as a museum in 2005.

7. THE PUMP HOUSE

This pub is one of the oldest buildings in Brighton, with cellars that date to medieval times.

Inside, a stone fireplace bears the initials of Miss Elliot, who bought the building in 1766 before it was converted into a pub around ten years later.

It acquired its name from an old timber pier featuring a pump house that was used to pump seawater ashore for bathing in the eighteenth century.

I was lucky enough to explore the damp cellars on my last visit with 'weeklyhistory'.

8. THE CRICKETERS

The oldest pub in Brighton, dating back to 1547, it was immortalised in Graham Greene's classic novel *Brighton Rock*. There is also a legend that it was where Jack the Ripper planned his notorious crimes.

Many historians believe Brighton local Robert Donston Stephenson is to blame for the string of bloody murders. He was a regular at the pub but travelled regularly to London, with the crimes lining up with his time in the capital.

These events no doubt contribute to its reputation as Brighton's most haunted pub, with poltergeists said to fling glasses and bottles throughout the bar.

N. THE LANES

Part of the original town settlement, they were built up throughout the eighteenth century before the area gained popularity following the construction of the Royal Pavilion and the Prince Regent's move to the area.

This labyrinth of narrow lanes is famous for its collection of small boutique and antique shops, and extends from North Street to Ship Street in the west, to East Street and Bartholomew Square in the south.

9. THE BLACK LION

Although ancient in appearance, this is a reconstruction of part of one of the oldest brewery buildings in the world.

The Black Lion brewery was established in 1546 by Deryk Carver, a Flemish immigrant. He was also landlord at the neighbouring Cricketers.

His religious conviction led to him being burned in a barrel outside the Star Inn at Lewes in 1555. After flinging his Bible into a crowd in defiance of the new Catholic ruler, he became the first Protestant to be martyred under Mary I.

The brewery, with its 54-foot well, was used by various brewers throughout the nineteenth century, but fell into disrepair and was demolished in 1968.

Today's pub was constructed in 1974, using many original flints and slates, as a replica of part of the brewery.

10. SEVEN STARS

Although the original licence dates to 1535, this Victorian-themed venue is notable as the birthplace of Brighton & Hove Albion Football Club.

On 24 June 1901, the then semi-professional football club was officially set up by former professional footballer John Jackson, who had been running the Farm Tavern in Hove.

It's one of the best pubs I've had the privilege to film, as the inside looks like the interior of the *Titanic* – with a raised seating area at the back, under a glass apex roof and surrounded by foliage.

11. VICTORY

Built in 1854, it is notable for its striking frontage featuring the original green tiling that was synonymous with Brighton brewer, Tamplins.

Many of the fittings are either original or from the 1910 refit and there are nods throughout to Admiral Lord Nelson and his famous ship.

Pub crawls are a great excuse to catch up with friends across the country. Here I grabbed a few drinks with Antonia, who is better known as gaming expert 8bit_bonello.

12. THE FORTUNE OF WAR

This beachside pub was built under the arches in 1882, and the interior is shaped like an upside-down boat. The name is a reference to the common slang term for a sailor with a wooden leg and/or an eye patch.

This is one of my favourite beachside pubs in the world and its location means it is one of the liveliest in the area, with fresh pizza and live music – although it's rare for the inside to be busy given the perfect location overlooking the beach.

This Londoner never misses the chance to paddle at the seaside, even if after 12 pubs the waves managed to soak me.

O. BEACH

Although a flat sandy area is exposed at low tide, the mainly shingle beach spans 5.4 miles as part of a total, unbroken 8-mile shoreline within the city limits.

The city council-owned beaches are divided into sections by groynes – which are large wooden structures perpendicular to the shore, with the intention of restricting the movement of sediment and limiting tidal damage. The first ones were built as early as 1724.

P. THE GRAND HOTEL

This iconic sea-front hotel was designed and built by architect John Whichcord Jr in 1864. Whichcord mostly designed office buildings in London, but is best known for his work here in Brighton.

In 1984 it was the location of an attempted assassination attempt on the prime minister at the time, Margaret Thatcher, by the Provisional Irish Republican Army (IRA).

The bomb had been concealed three weeks earlier behind a bath panel in room 629 and was detonated at 2.51 a.m., killing five people – among them Roberta Wakeman, wife of the chief whip, and a serving MP, Sir Anthony Berry.

Q. i360

The 531-foot observation tower was opened in 2016 and was designed, engineered and built by the team behind the London Eye.

The tall, needle-like structure has a capacity of two hundred people and was constructed at a cost of £46 million – hoping to attract 739,000 visitors each year.

It claimed to be the 'world's tallest moving observational tower' at its opening, however the world record was revoked after Guinness World Records were made aware of the 'Top o'Texas' tower which had opened three years earlier. They are, unfortunately, right when they say everything is bigger in Texas.

In 2021, Caterham Cars showcased their Seven 170 model in the observation pod, which did temporarily create the world's highest car showroom. So that's something.

R. WEST PIER

The first pier to be granted grade I listed status, it was designed by prolific seaside architect Eugenius Birch and opened in 1866. Its construction, during the boom period of pleasure beach building, was designed to bring tourists to the area.

It became the town's second pier and was extended in 1893, before a concert hall was added in 1916. As its popularity decreased, the pier was sold and the hall was replaced with a funfair, but increasing costs saw the owners file for bankruptcy.

It fell further into disrepair after closing to the public in 1975, with several sections collapsing into the sea during storms in 2002 and two suspected arson attacks in 2003 destroying most of the remaining structure. Nowadays, the gothic shell can be seen just offshore, watching the people of Brighton go about their lives, many of them unaware of its former glory.

BIRMINGHAM
(Jewellery Quarter to City)

England's second city hosts a wide variety of pubs, in converted theatres, spectacular canal-side venues and ornately decorated bars.

Its population exploded in the eighteenth century as it was hailed as the first major manufacturing town in the world, with a reputation for innovation and creativity.

Starting in the iconic jewellery quarter, the route skirts the city and takes in the famous canal system before heading into the city centre with its landmarks such as the library, cathedral and market squares.

What I love about this route is that the city often has a bad reputation for being boring, but its sheer scale means that there are so many things to see and do and (ideal for this book) an incredible number of pubs.

The Old Joint Stock, for example, is like no other pub you will see, and the city is worth visiting for this alone.

Start from Jewellery Quarter station (B18 6LE).

1. **The Rose Villa Tavern** *1.00 p.m.*
172 Warstone Lane, B18 6JW

2. **1000 Trades** *1.45 p.m.*
16 Frederick Street, B1 3HE

3. **The Shakespeare Inn** *2.30 p.m.*
31 Summer Row, B3 1JJ

4. **The Botanist** *3.15 p.m.*
12 Bridge Street, B1 2JR

5. **The Craven Arms** *4.00 p.m.*
47 Upper Gough Street, B1 1JG

6. **The Victoria** *4.45 p.m.*
48 John Bright Street, B1 1BN

7. **Bacchus Bar** *5.30 p.m.*
Burlington Arcade, New Street, B2 4JH

8. **The Trocadero** *6.30 p.m.*
Temple Street, B2 5BG

9. **The Old Joint Stock Pub & Theatre** *7.15 p.m.*
4 Temple Row West, B2 5NY

10. **The Colmore** *8.00 p.m.*
114–116 Colmore Row, B3 3BD

11. **Purecraft Bar & Kitchen** *8.45 p.m.*
30 Waterloo Street, B2 5TJ

12. **Post Office Vaults** *9.30 p.m.*
84 New Street, B2 4BA

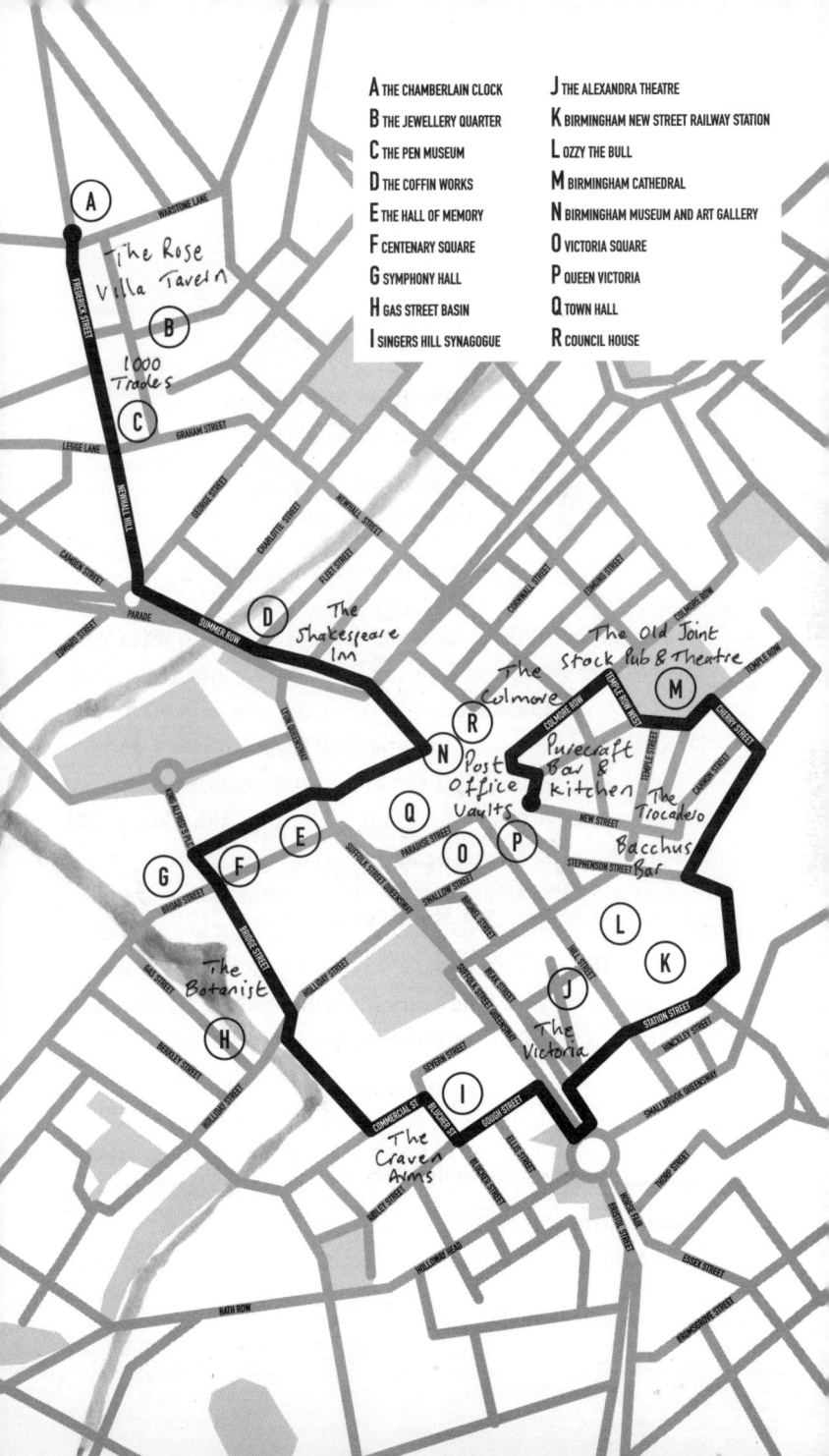

A THE CHAMBERLAIN CLOCK
B THE JEWELLERY QUARTER
C THE PEN MUSEUM
D THE COFFIN WORKS
E THE HALL OF MEMORY
F CENTENARY SQUARE
G SYMPHONY HALL
H GAS STREET BASIN
I SINGERS HILL SYNAGOGUE

J THE ALEXANDRA THEATRE
K BIRMINGHAM NEW STREET RAILWAY STATION
L OZZY THE BULL
M BIRMINGHAM CATHEDRAL
N BIRMINGHAM MUSEUM AND ART GALLERY
O VICTORIA SQUARE
P QUEEN VICTORIA
Q TOWN HALL
R COUNCIL HOUSE

DIRECTIONS

Turn right out of the station and follow the road to **Rose Villa Tavern (1)** on the roundabout, opposite the Chamberlain Clock **(A)**. Continue along Frederick Street **(B)** where **1000 Trades (2)** is on the left just before the Pen Museum **(C)**. Continue left, downhill, from the pub and follow the road left at the first major roundabout, over the canal, where the Coffin Works **(D)** is just before **The Shakespeare Inn (3)** on the corner.

Retrace a few steps back to cross the junction and follow the side of the main road before turning right at the Hall of Memory **(E)**, onto Centenary Square **(F)**, and then left before the Symphony Hall **(G)**, where **The Botanist (4, H)** is a short distance on the right, set back a little from the road.

Continue past the pub, taking the steps at the end of the road, just before the bridge to the right. Continue through the passage and past the retail spaces, turning left at the road and following it right past Singers Hill Synagogue **(I)**, where **The Craven Arms (5)** is on the corner.

Exit the pub down Gough Street and cross the main road at

the roundabout before heading back up and down the small alley to **The Victoria (6, J)**. Turn left from the pub and at the end of the road head immediately through New Street station **(K, L)** before emerging opposite the shopping centre where **Bacchus Bar (7)** is in the basement.

Pass through the shopping centre and turn left, before taking the first right onto Temple Street to **The Trocadero (8)**. At the end of the road past the pub, turn left and follow the edge of Birmingham Cathedral **(M)** where **The Old Joint Stock Pub & Theatre (9)** is opposite. Turning left from the pub, take a left at the next junction onto Colmore Row, where **The Colmore (10)** is on the left before the Birmingham Museum and Art Gallery **(N)** on Victoria Square **(O, P, Q)**. Around the corner is **Purecraft Bar & Kitchen (11)**, overlooking Council House **(R)** with **Post Office Vaults (12)** a short distance along the tram lines.

---

1. THE ROSE VILLA TAVERN

At the heart of the jewellery quarter, this iconic pub was built by Mitchells & Butler brewery's preferred architects, Wood & Kendrick, in 1920.

The grade II listed pub is on CAMRA's heritage list and has retained the original tiling and beautiful stained-glass windows.

It's hard to imagine such a glorious-looking pub, containing so many unique features, sitting so inconspicuously on the edge of a roundabout – making it a fabulous place to start.

A. THE CHAMBERLAIN CLOCK

This icon of the jewellery quarter was erected in 1903 to mark the radical liberalist Joseph Chamberlain's tour of South Africa after the end of the Second Boer War and was originally powered by a wind-up mechanism.

Chamberlain had been a resident on Frederick Street, where the clock sits, and he was notable for his efforts to abolish Plate Duties tax, which affected local tradesmen.

B. THE JEWELLERY QUARTER

Producing around 40 per cent of all jewellery made in the UK, the area is Europe's largest concentration of businesses involved in the jewellery trade. It also, unsurprisingly, houses the world's largest assay office, which is responsible for hallmarking around 12 million items a year.

There are records of there having been at least twenty-six jewellers in the area as far back as 1780, and over the next 150 years the industry grew to supply over half of the gold and jewellery products sold in London, and a significant portion of the rest of the UK.

Most jewellers worked in small, independent shops employing between five and fifty people. As workers often lived alongside their shops, the area remained residential despite the growth of industrial buildings. The large population in the area meant the council had to improve public services in various ways, such as providing parks and cemeteries, and laying gas pipes.

Having survived an economic downturn in the 1880s, the area received widespread support from the local council for over a century to regenerate the area and industry.

Many of the buildings are protected due to their age or historical significance. This has become a more pressing issue in recent years due to the sharp increase in tourism to the area following the success of the TV series *Peaky Blinders*.

2. 1000 TRADES

The bowing, exposed-brick walls honour the building's history; it was a nineteenth-century jewellery workshop before being converted into a badge factory, split across three floors.

They still honour the old use of the building, covering a large wall in pins from all over the world, and will accept new pins from visitors to this day.

C. THE PEN MUSEUM

Run by the Birmingham Pen Trade Heritage Association, Birmingham's steel pen trade is showcased in this museum, which was opened in 2001.

Throughout the nineteenth century around a hundred companies distributed steel pens in the area before the nibs were replaced with fountain and ballpoint pens.

D. THE COFFIN WORKS

Housed in the Newman Brothers Coffin Furniture Factory, this macabre museum was opened in 2014 as an attempt to save the grade II* listed building.

Originally a brass foundry company, the Newman brothers moved to the location in 1894 and immediately switched to producing coffin furniture such as handles, crucifixes and nameplates, as well as soft furnishings such as gowns, shrouds, linings and cushions.

Throughout its operation it became known for high-quality craftsmanship and was used for the funerals of Sir Winston Churchill, George V, George VI, the Queen Mother and Princess Diana.

Its glory years in the 1960s were followed by a decline in trade, largely caused by an increase in cremations and the outlawing of the use of metal in coffin making.

While it continues to produce high-end brass fittings, the company officially shut down in 1998.

The building fell into disrepair and it was not until 2006, when the Birmingham Conservation Trust secured £1.5 million in funding, that the area was saved from redevelopment.

The museum features three main areas, showcasing the stamp room (where breastplates and handles were produced), the shroud room (where linings and shrouds were made) and the warehouse.

3. THE SHAKESPEARE INN

Built in the late nineteenth century, its distinctive beer garden is one of the few in the immediate area, among the more recent university developments.

Over time the ramshackle building has been developed in stages; there is a modern toilet block that looks very much out of place.

E. THE HALL OF MEMORY

This war memorial was erected in 1925 to commemorate the 12,320 Birmingham residents who died in World War I.

It was constructed as the first part of a civic planning scheme to create new council offices, a mayoral residence and a public library, but the project was abandoned at the outbreak of World War II.

It survived the surrounding devastation caused during the night of the Birmingham Blitz on 11 December 1940, which destroyed St Thomas' Church and many of the adjacent buildings.

F. CENTENARY SQUARE

Named in 1989 to commemorate the centenary of Birmingham's ascension to city status, the area was purchased in the 1920s to create a hub for government services.

These days it is the main staging area for significant events such as the German Christmas markets, Remembrance Day services, New Year celebrations, and arts and music festivals, often hosting attractions such as an observation wheel or an ice rink. In the summer there is also a water installation in which children are allowed to play.

G. SYMPHONY HALL

This innovative hall was designed by Percy Thomas Partnership and opened by Queen Elizabeth II in 1991 at a cost of £30 million.

Its interior is modelled on the Musikverein in Vienna and Amsterdam's Concertgebouw.

It hosts around 270 events each year, with the hall's acoustic flexibility being a particularly distinctive feature. There is a reverberation chamber behind the stage and along the sides of the hall, which adds 50 per cent to its volume.

Being built only 100 feet from the railway line, it is mounted on rubber cushions to prevent the transmission of vibrations.

4. THE BOTANIST

Formerly the James Brindley, the exterior resembles a large warehouse and it sits overlooking Gas Street Basin.

It was originally built in the 1980s and closed as the area underwent regeneration, before reopening in 2017 as the Canal House. The Botanist is best known for interesting cocktails and its famous hanging kebabs.

When the sun is shining this is one of the best places in the city to sit and enjoy a cold beer at the water's edge.

H. GAS STREET BASIN

The start of the Birmingham Canal, which was completed in 1773, the basin acts as a barrier to prevent the Birmingham and Worcester canals from benefiting from each other's water.

It has made several appearances on-screen, having featured in Cliff Richard's film *Take Me High*, and soap opera *Crossroads*.

Although much of the area was redeveloped in the 1990s, many of the buildings remain grade II listed.

5. THE CRAVEN ARMS

This Holder's Brewery pub was built in the early nineteenth century and has retained its striking original frontage.

What I love about this pub is that it is one of those genuine hidden gems that are off the beaten track. It has hardly any online presence, and a welcoming group of locals who were happy to share tips about exploring the city.

Look out for the homemade cheese rolls behind the bar!

A bizarre sight among the modern developments on the outskirts of the city.

I. SINGERS HILL SYNAGOGUE

The congregation here dates to 1780, and first worshipped in a nearby area known as the Froggery.

It then moved several times over the years before settling when the current building was completed in 1856. The design features a 'Norman wheel window' and combines classical revival, Romanesque revival and Italianate details.

6. THE VICTORIA

Popular with audiences at the neighbouring Alexandra Theatre, it has a reputation as a LGBTQ+ venue. It also hosts live music on occasion.

It is believed that the pub is haunted and, on my last visit, the barman showed us where he had his first ghostly encounter; he isn't alone, as several locals believe they have seen a shadowy presence leaning against the end of the bar.

J. THE ALEXANDRA THEATRE

Affectionately known as 'the Alex', this unremarkable building was completed in 1901 and opened as the Lyceum Theatre.

After a disappointing opening show it was sold and renamed the Alexandra, by Lester Collingwood, in 1902.

There is a sinister history of hauntings, with many people dying in tragic circumstances in the building. Collingwood himself was killed in a traffic accident and the subsequent owner, Leon Salberg, died in his office.

It is also said that the ghost of a woman dressed in grey roams the building, although it is unclear who she could be. Tragically, this is the location where actor Arthur Lowe, of *Dad's Army* fame, collapsed in his dressing room before dying of a stroke shortly after in 1982.

K. BIRMINGHAM NEW STREET RAILWAY STATION

The largest and busiest of the Birmingham stations, it is the eleventh busiest in the UK, with more than 30 million entries and exits a year. It is also the busiest interchange station, with more than 4 million annual changes.

At the time of its opening, in 1854, it had the largest single-span arched roof in the world. However, it has since been extensively revamped, both in the 1960s and in 2015.

L. OZZY THE BULL

The centrepiece from the 2022 Commonwealth Games was rehomed inside the station a year later. Then named the Raging Bull, he represented the city's industrial past at the climax of the opening ceremony.

He is not to be confused with the bronze sculpture *The Bull* that guards the main entrance of the Bull Ring shopping centre. *The Bull* is much smaller, and is often dressed to reflect goings-on in the city at various times.

Ozzy the mechanical bull.

7. BACCHUS BAR

Beneath the former Midland Railway Hotel, the catacombs of this pub are separated into distinctive historically themed rooms. The building blends Roman mosaics with Greek friezes, medieval armour and Egyptian tombs.

Beneath one of Birmingham's oldest streets, dating back to 1398, this was a regular pre-drink stop for visitors to the Theatre Royal, which was demolished in 1956.

It has a somewhat salubrious reputation as 'the affairs pub', as its hidden location and nooks and crannies were said to make it the perfect location to sneak a drink with a lover before parting at the station.

8. THE TROCADERO

This grade II listed former fire station was built in 1846 and altered less than fifty years later into the Bodega wine bar; a distinctive skylight shows where the pole used to be located.

The wine bar's former landlord, Henry Skinner, was said to have been murdered in 1895 after a dispute with two local brothers.

The colourful glazed front was installed in 1902, after which it became the Trocadero – known affectionately as 'the Troc'.

M. BIRMINGHAM CATHEDRAL

This baroque parish church was consecrated in 1715 and sits at the heart of the city centre. The organ still contains some original parts dating back to its opening. Its high point is said to be at the same level as the cross on London's St Paul's Cathedral.

As the congregation of the nearby St Martin in the Bull Ring grew, it became clear a bigger venue was needed. The increasing pressure to find a new home eventually led to the construction of St Philip's Church on land donated by Robert Philips. It was completed at a cost of £5,012 – only £990,000 in today's money. It became a cathedral in 1905.

It was gutted during World War II bombing, although many of the most precious treasures and windows had been removed at the start of the war.

The bells ceased to chime in 1906 due to safety concerns about the stability of the tower, but subsequent restoration work has completed the twelve bells that exist today. The largest of these – the tenor bell – weighs 1,584 kilograms and is in the key of D.

Cathedral of St Philip

9. THE OLD JOINT STOCK PUB & THEATRE

Built in 1862 and originally designed as a library, this grade II listed building was quickly converted into a branch of the bank that lent it its name – before it was taken over by Lloyds Bank in 1889.

It was not until 1997 that the building was converted into a pub, with a ninety-five-seat theatre opening, after a £350,000 refurbishment, in 2006. Its location near the financial district of Birmingham makes it popular for after-work drinks and corporate lunches, so you can often see people in suits coming and going.

10. THE COLMORE

Another former branch of Lloyds Bank, it was converted in 2019 with an opulent style based on the exclusive bars of New York City.

It is located on Colmore Row, which was designated a conservation area in 1971 and contains twenty-three listed buildings.

While the original buildings were in a typical eighteenth-century brick and stucco Georgian style, they were replaced between 1870 and 1900 by the distinctive Victorian premises that remain today.

Much of the road was due to be widened to form the inner ring road system after World War II, but conservation action to prevent the demolition of several buildings resulted in a change of plans.

N. BIRMINGHAM MUSEUM AND ART GALLERY

Run by the largest independent museum trust in the UK, the Birmingham Museum Trust, which manages eight others across the city.

It houses more than 800,000 objects, in mostly free-to-access galleries, and includes artwork from the likes of John Constable, coin collections from the Middle Ages, and the Sultanganj Buddha – the largest complete copper figure remaining of its age, from around AD 500–700.

The current gallery was opened in 1885 following donations equivalent to £1.1 million in today's money.

After bombing in World War II, it required extensive repair work, with seven galleries undergoing restoration.

O. VICTORIA SQUARE

This central square was unremarkably named Council House Square until 1901, when it was renamed to honour Queen Victoria, just twelve days before her death.

The area was cleared and repurposed when Christ Church was demolished in 1899 and more than six hundred bodies needed to be excavated and moved from the grounds into Warstone Lane Cemetery. The office and retail buildings that now populate the area were constructed shortly afterwards.

In the 1970s the unsightly buildings were demolished to make way for an open, pedestrianised space that created a public focal point in the area.

The square contains several sculptures, including a bronze of Queen Victoria and Antony Gormley's *Iron:Man*.

The most prominent feature is *The River* by Indian sculptor Dhruva Mistry, which is colloquially known as the *Floozie in the Jacuzzi*. It was unveiled in 1994 by Princess Diana, however it encountered structural issues due to continually leaking and was switched off in 2013 to save costs; it was refurbished ahead of the Commonwealth Games in 2022.

The fountain features an almost 10-foot-tall bronze statue of a woman, with two Darley Dale stone sculptures – known as Guardians – either side of the fountain.

Every Christmas the square forms the focal point for the German Christmas market, with a stage for live music and a carousel.

Victoria Square

P. QUEEN VICTORIA

Her reign of 63 years and 216 days – the longest of any British monarch until Elizabeth II – constituted the Victorian era, which was a significant period of industrial, political, scientific and military change within the UK.

During her reign the British Empire expanded considerably, and she was granted the title Empress of India in 1876.

The queen first visited Birmingham as a child and described the area as 'desolate' and 'black'. Once crowned, she visited multiple times, notably in 1858 and 1887, although we do not know how she felt about the second city by this point. The city must have changed a lot since her childhood, as I can't help but disagree with her opinion on this one.

Q. TOWN HALL

The first significant work of the nineteenth century in the style of Roman Revival architecture, it is based on the Temple of Castor and Pollux in the Roman Forum. Designed by the inventor of the hansom cab, Joseph Hansom, and Edward Welch, construction began in the spring of 1832 and was completed two and a half years later.

The build was severely disrupted due to Hansom tendering too low and going bankrupt, and then delayed further by the death of two construction workers – Badger and Heap, whose memorial rests in the cathedral grounds – when a crane collapsed.

It houses what was at the time one of the largest and most technically advanced concert pipe organs in the world, with more than six thousand pipes, which was installed by William Hill & Sons in 1834.

Christmas 1853 saw Charles Dickens give the first public readings of his work in the building and it has showcased many prominent events as a music venue, hosting gigs by Buddy Holly, the Rolling Stones, the Beatles and Bob Dylan.

11. PURECRAFT BAR & KITCHEN

The first bar owned by Purity Brewing Co was opened in 2014 and was part of then Prince Charles's route to the Commonwealth Games events in 2022.

I love to include a mix of places on the pub crawls, so while this might not be an old establishment it is a great place, with a different vibe from the historic buildings on this route, and a great selection of beers and ales.

R. COUNCIL HOUSE

Located in its own postcode, this classical-style building is the home of the city council, local government and the lord mayor's office.

Completed in 1874, plans were made as early as 1852 when the local administration outgrew their contemporary location on Moor Street.

It features a large clock tower that is affectionately known as Big Brum and was part of the first extension of the building shortly after its construction.

12. POST OFFICE VAULTS

A single red door leads to this subterranean bar, which is renowned for its encyclopaedic coverage of craft beers from across the world.

It's easy to assume places like this are filled with 'weird beard' real-ale lovers, but this popular venue is raw, rough and great fun. At the end of the crawl, my camera assistant Maddie and I stuck around for a good few drinks.

A well-deserved drink for Maddie and me at the end of a long day filming the route for our social media.

LIVERPOOL
(Cathedral to Brewery Village)

Starting in St George's Quarter before looping past the two distinctly different cathedrals in the city, this route passes some of the most beautiful and iconic pubs anywhere in the UK.

At times Liverpool can feel like it's in a bubble from the rest of the UK, as its mix of Irish heritage and fierce football passion results in it being one of the friendliest cities I've visited.

It is worth the journey for the Philharmonic Dining Rooms alone, but this route also includes more intimate local venues before ending at the heart of the historic brewery buildings that underpinned the construction of the city's pubs.

Start at Lime Street station (L1 1JD).

1. **The Crown Hotel** *1.00 p.m.*
43 Lime Street, L1 1JQ

2. **The Vines** *1.30 p.m.*
81 Lime Street, L1 1JQ

3. **Roscoe Head** *2.15 p.m.*
24 Roscoe Street, L1 2SX

4. **The Pen Factory** *3.00 p.m.*
13 Hope Street, L1 9BQ

5. **The Philharmonic Dining Rooms** *3.30 p.m.*
36 Hope Street, L1 9BX

6. **Ye Cracke** *4.15 p.m.*
13 Rice Street, L1 9BB

7. **The Grapes** *5.00 p.m.*
60 Roscoe Street, L1 9DW

8. **Peter Kavanagh's** *5.45 p.m.*
2–6 Egerton Street, L8 7LY

9. **Yellow Submarine** *6.45 p.m.*
70 Stanhope Street, L8 5RF

10. **The Brewery Tap** *7.30 p.m.*
39 Stanhope Street, L8 5RE

11. **Punch Tarmey's** *8.00 p.m.*
31 Grafton Street, Cains Brewery Village, L8 5SD

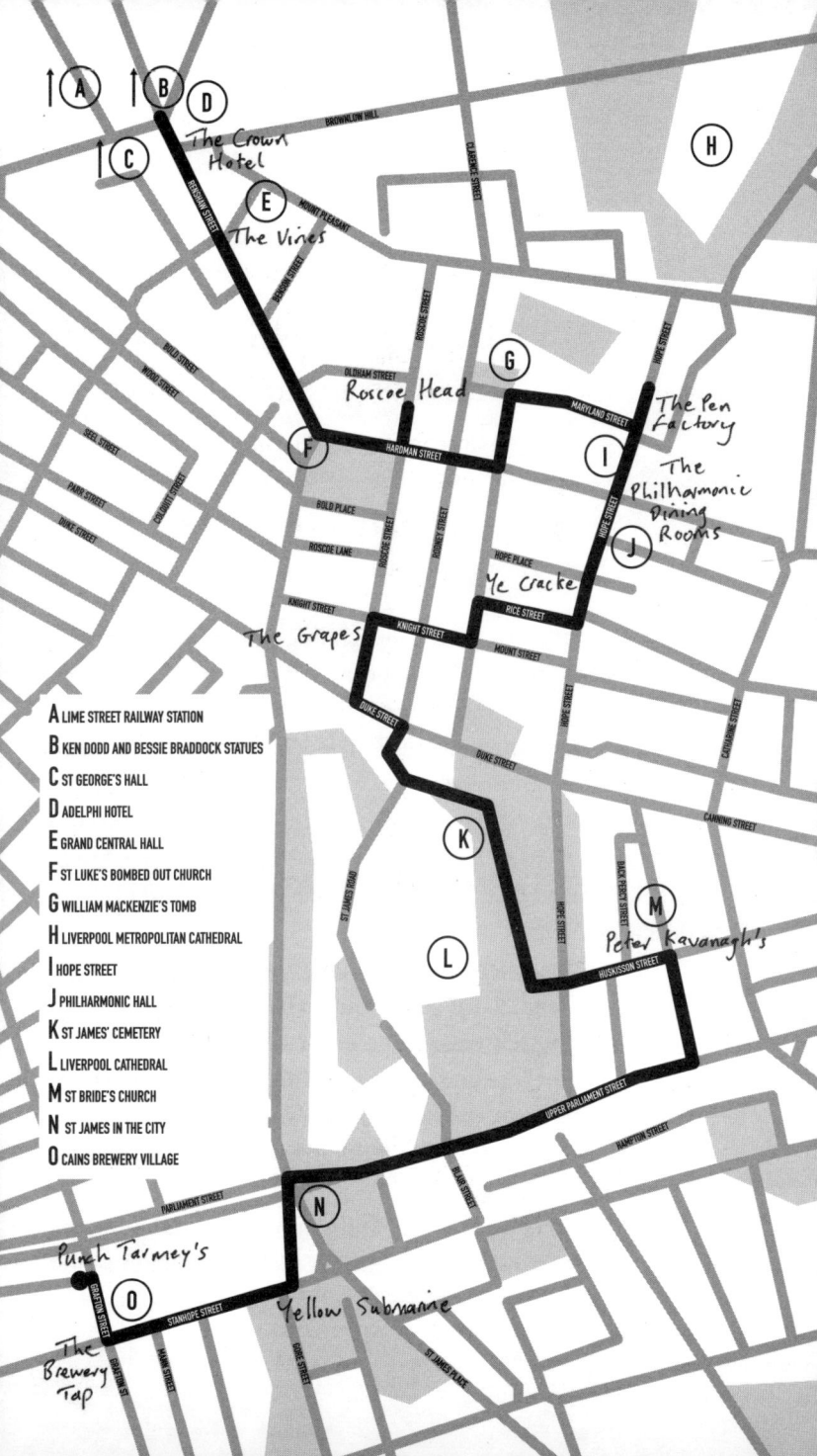

A LIME STREET RAILWAY STATION
B KEN DODD AND BESSIE BRADDOCK STATUES
C ST GEORGE'S HALL
D ADELPHI HOTEL
E GRAND CENTRAL HALL
F ST LUKE'S BOMBED OUT CHURCH
G WILLIAM MACKENZIE'S TOMB
H LIVERPOOL METROPOLITAN CATHEDRAL
I HOPE STREET
J PHILHARMONIC HALL
K ST JAMES' CEMETERY
L LIVERPOOL CATHEDRAL
M ST BRIDE'S CHURCH
N ST JAMES IN THE CITY
O CAINS BREWERY VILLAGE

The Crown Hotel
The Vines
Roscoe Head
The Pen Factory
The Philharmonic Dining Rooms
Ye Cracke
The Grapes
Peter Kavanagh's
Punch Tarmey's
The Brewery Tap
Yellow Submarine

DIRECTIONS

Leave the station **(A, B)** and, depending on the exit, either turn left with St George's Hall opposite **(C)** or head directly onto Lime Street where **The Crown Hotel (1)** is on the corner. Continue left from the pub where **The Vines (2)** is on the next corner of the same block.

Continue along the same road, past the Adelphi Hotel **(D)** and Grand Central Hall **(E)** before turning left adjacent to St Luke's Bombed Out Church **(F)** where **Roscoe Head (3)** is on the corner of the first left.

Stay on the main road, and take the first left then right down Maryland Street past William Mackenzie's Tomb **(G)** before turning left onto Hope Street under the gaze of the Metropolitan Cathedral **(H)** where **The Pen Factory (4)** is a few doors up. Leave the pub and walk away from the cathedral along Hope Street **(I)** to **The Philharmonic Dining Rooms (5)** at the end of the road.

Cross the road, past the Philharmonic Hall **(J)** and turn right along narrow Rice Street to **Ye Cracke (6)**. Continue past the pub, turning left at the junction before turning right along Mount Street where **The Grapes (7)** is on the corner, a couple of blocks along.

Leave the pub and head south, turning right at the main road and heading through St James' Cemetery **(K)** at the back of Liverpool Cathedral **(L)**, heading across the park and following Huskisson Street, which lines up with the south end of the building. Go past St Bride's Church **(M)** and on to **Peter Kavanagh's (8)**, which is right then left past the church.

Turn left at the pub back to the road, then turn left to the main road, before following it right past St James in the City **(N)**, after which turn left and then over the road to the **Yellow Submarine (9)** at the edge of Cains Brewery Village **(O)**, where **The Brewery Tap (10)** and **Punch Tarmey's (11)** are on the corners of the next block.

A. LIME STREET RAILWAY STATION

This end-of-the-line station is the oldest grand terminus in the world, opened in the summer of 1836, although it has undergone frequent updates and extensions.

Upon completion in 1867, the northern arch was the largest such structure in the world, with a total span of 200 feet.

During the early twentieth century there were four large railway companies: Great Western; London, Midland and Scottish; London and North Eastern; and Southern. They were under state control during World War I; however, it was not until 1948 that ownership was nationalised under Clement Attlee's Labour government.

B. KEN DODD AND BESSIE BRADDOCK STATUES

Found on the station concourse, this installation by Tom Murphy is called *Chance Meeting* and was created to recognise two of Liverpool's most iconic figures. Murphy is a self-taught sculptor, best known for his work in bronze.

Ken Dodd's entertainment career started in the mid-1950s and typically contained lively verbal and physical comedy routines, often including his 'tickling stick' prop – a large feather duster.

He was born in Knotty Ash – the suburb of Liverpool that is the origin of the Diddymen, a mythical race of little people who were popularised by Dodd.

Dodd's surreal style of humour would often reference the fictional jam butty mines and the black pudding plantations. He was visually striking; his distinctive buck teeth were a result of a cycling accident as a child.

Politician Bessie Braddock was the first woman to be granted the Freedom of the City of Liverpool and is best remembered for her combative personality as a left-wing councillor when campaigning on housing, public health and wider social issues.

Although never officially holding office in government, she was a member of the Liverpool council for over thirty years before serving as an MP for Liverpool Exchange between 1945 and 1970.

She died in 1971, shortly after the 1970 general election, in which the Conservatives won a surprise victory. She was particularly appreciated in Liverpool where she earned the nickname 'Battling Bessie'.

C. ST GEORGE'S HALL

This grade I listed neoclassical building contains concert halls and local law courts, and was constructed between 1841 and 1854.

The elaborate interior is notable as the first attempt to create air conditioning in a public building in the UK. The system drew air through two shafts that were heated by hot-water pipes during cold weather and used the opposite approach with cold-water pipes and small fountains during hotter seasons.

The building is surrounded by many statues and elaborate designs, including a tribute to former prime minister Benjamin Disraeli on the eastern steps, and one to Major General William Earle at the south-east corner.

The halls have hosted many events since the first visit of Queen Victoria in 1851, and the small concert room regularly hosted readings by Charles Dickens.

Its plateau is often used for public rallies and protests, as well as gatherings on the death of Beatles John Lennon and George Harrison, and victory parades for the Liverpool and Everton football teams.

The exterior has featured in several movies, including *In the Name of the Father* and *The Batman*, and TV series such as *Peaky Blinders* and *The War of the Worlds*.

1. THE CROWN HOTEL

This Art Nouveau-style building was constructed in 1905 and retains many of its original features, such as ornate plaster-work ceilings, and push bells behind the seats for patrons to order table service.

The opulence of this Walkers Ales pub is likely born out of competition with the similarly spectacular Philharmonic.

A mischievous decorator hid six cigars in the intricate ceiling – can you spot them all?

2. THE VINES

This Edwardian masterpiece was built in 1907 on the site of an 1867 pub opened by Albert B. Vines. It is affectionately nicknamed 'The Big House' by its patrons.

Its flamboyant style is thanks to local brewer Robert Cain and architect Walter Thomas – the plasterwork, which depicts a harvest scene, was created by sculptor Walter Gilbert, and the pub incorporates other works by Henry Gustave Hiller.

Do not forget to walk to the rear of the pub and catch the spectacular rear bar under an impressive skylight.

Possibly the most impressed I've been walking into a pub and seeing this startling room.

D. ADELPHI HOTEL

The current building is the third iteration of this railway hotel, and the grade II listed building contains more than four hundred rooms.

The original hotel from 1826 was replaced in 1876, with the latter being purchased by Midland Railway at the end of the nineteenth century.

It once had a set of heated tanks in the basement which were used to store live turtles for its speciality turtle soup.

As Liverpool became a major departure point for ocean-going liners, the hotel grew in popularity – especially with wealthy passengers. Although it never actually visited the port, the *Titanic* was registered in Liverpool and the Sefton Suite of the hotel is said to perfectly replicate the liner's first-class smoking lounge.

E. GRAND CENTRAL HALL

Designed by Bolton architects Bradshaw Gass & Hope, this live music venue has a capacity of 3,576 people and was originally opened as the Central Hall of the Wesleyan Mission in 1905.

The Wesleyan Mission was a Methodist movement that lasted from around the 1730s until 1932, when it was combined with the Primitive and United Methodist Churches.

F. ST LUKE'S BOMBED OUT CHURCH

Built over twenty years from 1811, the church was almost destroyed during the Blitz in 1941, with its now roofless shell giving it its current moniker.

Most of the original features, such as the aisles, nave and ornate ceiling, were destroyed, as well as the stained-glass windows.

As it has remained structurally sound, the building has remained as a tribute to those lost in the war and features a sculpture of the 1914 Christmas truce football match, called *All Together Now*, by Andy Edwards.

The bombed out church is a fitting tribute to the city's defiance against war.

3. ROSCOE HEAD

One of Liverpool's oldest pubs, having opened in 1830, it is the only pub in the north of England to have appeared in every edition of CAMRA's *Good Beer Guide*.

It's a classic, old-school pub with almost no social media or online presence.

G. WILLIAM MACKENZIE'S TOMB

This unusual, pyramid-shaped tomb was erected around the grave of Anglo-Scottish engineer William Mackenzie, who was regarded as one of the leading civil engineering contractors of the 1840s.

The tomb of the eccentric engineer has been the topic of discussion for years, with the pointed memorial said to be a portal to the spirit world.

Other rumours state that the ground underneath it contains a labyrinth of tunnels that stretch underneath the city. The most sinister legend is that the charismatic Mackenzie sold his soul to the devil over a game of poker in exchange for power and wealth.

Upon his death he is said to have been placed upright, holding a winning hand of cards, in the belief that the devil could not come to collect his dues because the engineer had never been 'laid to rest'.

H. LIVERPOOL METROPOLITAN CATHEDRAL

Liverpool was a major destination for immigrants during the Great Irish Famine that lasted from 1845 to 1852, and the local population exploded. With around half a million Irish Catholics fleeing to England, the local diocese was compelled to build a new cathedral. The 'Lady Chapel' of the cathedral was completed by 1856, but then the project stalled due to funding issues; it was demolished in 1980.

Planning for the current building began in the 1930s, and it was intended to be the largest church in the world, with a dome that would have stood over 30 feet taller than that of St Peter's Basilica in the Vatican.

Although work commenced, the impact of World War II and rising costs left it unfinished, with only the crypt completed.

After alternative efforts also fell through, the current iteration was designed in 1959 by Sir Frederick Gibberd. Gibberd is best known as the creator of the prefabricated steel-framed house that was common after the war.

His distinctive vision created a concrete conical structure, surrounded by thirteen individual chapels with boomerang-shaped trusses and flying buttresses giving the cathedral a tent-like appearance.

Likely due to the limited budget and speed of construction, the finished building suffered several structural problems – including leaks and broken tiles – leading to the cathedral's governing body suing Gibberd for £1.3 million.

Liverpool Metropolitan Cathedral

4. THE PEN FACTORY

This lively pub and bistro features a wonderful beer garden, and is popular among theatregoers attending shows at the nearby Everyman Theatre.

The building – as the name suggests – was originally the country's sole manufacturer of eighteen-carat gold pen nibs. It was the only factory in an area better known for its impressive homes. It was reopened at the end of 2024 and comes strongly recommended by my friend Kam, who runs the hugely popular

'beerguideworldwide' social media accounts. Upon entry, be
sure to check out the orange steel door to the right, behind
which was the safe to store the gold used in the nibs' manu-
facture.

I. HOPE STREET

Taking its name from a former local merchant, William Hope,
whose house was on the site of the Philharmonic Hall, it is
recognised as one of Liverpool's 'great streets' and was voted
as the best in the UK and Ireland by the non-profit Academy
of Urbanism.

5. THE PHILHARMONIC DINING ROOMS

Often regarded as the most ornate pub in England, it took two
years to build from 1898 and was designed by local architect
Walter Thomas for brewer Robert Cain.

The exterior is constructed in ashlar stone and features elaborate architraves, a two-storey oriel window (a protruding bay
window) and a low relief carving of musical instruments and
musicians.

Spread over five floors, the rooms are decorated with a
musical theme and it has hosted the likes of Buddy Holly and
Paul McCartney; it was even rumoured to be John Lennon's
favourite pub.

Its name comes from the adjacent Philharmonic Hall and,
as well as metal gates that are some of the finest Art Nouveau
examples in the country, it is famous for its extravagant gents'
toilets, which showcase pink-marble basins and matching
imitation-marble urinals.

At the start of 2020 it became the first purpose-built pub to be granted grade I listed status.

It was the most requested pub from followers on my social media channels and is regularly touted as being the UK's most beautiful.

When you walk into this ornate pub it's hard to believe that the most famous part is the rose marble toilets.

J. PHILHARMONIC HALL

This iconic venue was opened in 1939, after the original 1849 building was destroyed in a 1933 fire.

Although the efforts of more than a hundred firefighters were unable to prevent the devastation, a fireproof safe ensured the survival of several autographed pictures and some instruments.

The replacement building was planned in controversial circumstances, as the council demanded the auditorium be capable of both cinema and theatre use. Theatre purists at the time felt that the new 'movies' were a passing fad, and would hurt the potential longevity of the theatre.

The new building has capacity for 1,700 visitors, and stages more than 250 events each year – classical music concerts account for more than 20 per cent of them.

6. YE CRACKE

A popular local for John Lennon and his first wife, Cynthia, this pub opened in 1825. It takes its name from the Liverpudlian slang for an alleyway, which is apt given its location on a narrow offshoot from Hope Street.

It was also where Lennon and Stuart Sutcliffe, the original bassist for the Beatles, came up with the band's name, having taken inspiration from Buddy Holly's 'Crickets'. The original spelling was thought to be 'Beetles'.

Sutcliffe is one of a handful of people referred to as 'the fifth Beatle'; he died from a brain haemorrhage at the age of twenty-one in Hamburg, Germany. Some others include George Martin (who helped produce and compose early Beatles albums), Brian Epstein (the man who discovered them) and Neil Aspinall (their road manager).

The pub is also thought to be where locals made plans during the Boer War.

7. THE GRAPES

This tiny pub was originally called the Little Grapes and dates from 1804, making it one of the city's oldest.

It dropped the 'little' from its name after a major refurbishment during 2016. I understand this change, as I can't think of anybody who would want to advertise the fact that their grapes are little.

K. ST JAMES' CEMETERY

This is the site of a former stone quarry that operated from the sixteenth century until it was exhausted in 1825, and was also the location of a chalybeate spring – natural mineral waters that contain iron.

The cemetery's layout is based on the famous Père Lachaise Cemetery in Paris, which is the final resting place of the likes of Oscar Wilde, Edith Piaf, Chopin and Jim Morrison.

St James' features a windowless oratory, in the style of a Greek Doric temple, which accommodated funerals ahead of a burial in the cemetery.

After 57,774 burials in just over a century of existence, it was closed in 1936 and fell into a state of disrepair before 1972 efforts removed many of the tombstones and turned the area into a public park.

L. LIVERPOOL CATHEDRAL

Constructed between 1904 and 1978, it holds many records and features in several top ten lists due to its scale.

As the largest religious building in the UK, it is also the longest cathedral in the world. It is the eighth-largest church in the world, the fifth-largest cathedral by volume in the world and one of the tallest non-spired church buildings in the world.

A competition was held in 1901 to design the new cathedral, and it was won, two years later, by the then twenty-two-year-old Sir Giles Gilbert Scott – who was also responsible for Battersea Power Station, the New Bodleian Library in Oxford and red telephone boxes – with King Edward VII laying the foundation stone in 1904.

Although the original design was to feature two towers at

the west end, a redesign to a single erection in 1910 forced the
cathedral committee to intervene and call for detailed plans
that took over a year to pass. Luckily, this did not halt construction for ever and the building was completed.

The impressive height of Liverpool Cathedral often sees it covered in fog – or, as the locals call it, 'scouse mist'.

M. ST BRIDE'S CHURCH

This temple-like structure was completed in 1830 and is the
best surviving neoclassical church in Liverpool.

It features a monument to a couple who lost their lives
when the paddle steamer *Rothesay Castle* ran aground in the
Great Orme in 1831. This was due to several factors, including a drunken captain, bad weather and a lack of suitable life-
boats, which led to the drowning of 130 people.

8. PETER KAVANAGH'S

A previous winner of CAMRA's Pub of the Year, in 1929 the
walls were adorned with murals by Scottish painter Eric Rob-
inson, who based the work on Charles Dickens's *The Pickwick
Papers* for the Pickwick Room and William Hogarth's draw-
ings for the Hogarth Room.

It was originally built in 1844, and became a licensed premises ten years later. After being known as the Liver, the Liver Hotel, the Grapes and Peter's Hotel over the years, it was renamed in 1978 to honour Peter Kavanagh, who held the licence from 1897 to 1950.

I was joined by craft beer expert Kam of 'beerguideworldwide' and we sat down with the pub's landlady of over thirty years, Rita, who regaled us with stories from the pub as well as making us laugh about her reluctance to serve lager and lime as she 'doesn't serve cocktails'!

N. ST JAMES IN THE CITY

This Georgian-style church was built in 1774 and operated for two hundred years before being declared redundant and falling into disrepair.

It was reopened in 2010, with the congregation sheltered under a marquee due to the poor condition of the roof. It is also known for being the oldest remaining building in Britain constructed with cast-iron columns. Nowadays, it is known for a diverse congregation, with many people of Caribbean and West African heritage attending. This diversity is not new, as the church was once one of the only churches in the city that allowed enslaved people to worship.

9. YELLOW SUBMARINE

Named after the 1966 Beatles song that was issued on a double A-side with 'Eleanor Rigby' and performed by Ringo Starr, this bar encapsulates a lot of the whimsy from that track.

The song inspired the animated film of the same name

around two years later and its US release coincided with John Lennon's controversial remarks that the Beatles were 'more popular than Jesus', which led to several radio bans.

The submarine that hosts the bar was originally a prop in the Sean Connery film *The Hunt for Red October* before it was purchased from Paramount Studios and used as a floating hotel on the Albert Dock – where it entertained the likes of boxers Lennox Lewis and Mike Tyson, as well as musician Nick Rhodes and actor Tony Curtis.

O. CAINS BREWERY VILLAGE

Founded by Robert Cain in 1858, Cains brewery merged with the Warrington-based Peter Walker & Son in 1921 to form the larger Walker Cain brewery.

Irishman Cain had begun brewing at just twenty-four years old, and opened his own pub before growing his empire to include more than two hundred in the next twenty-five years – including the famous Philharmonic Dining Rooms and the Vines.

After passing through several owners, including Boddingtons, the area was earmarked for redevelopment. There is still a small brewery on-site, along with housing and leisure facilities.

10. THE BREWERY TAP

Housed inside Robert Cain's former Mersey brewery, it sits at the heart of the terracotta buildings of the Brewery Village.

While small compared to its neighbour, Punch Tarmey's, the pub is notable as the first one constructed by Cains brewery.

11. PUNCH TARMEY'S

Liverpool's largest Irish pub, its name comes from the owner's bare-knuckle-fighting great-grandfather's nickname.

Legend has it that the fighter won a Dublin tournament and received two ferry tickets to Liverpool and a cash prize equivalent to £250 in today's money.

Together with his eighteen-year-old wife, he set sail to Merseyside where he spent time working in the pits and supplementing his income with further fights.

The pub contains five bars and can easily accommodate more than a thousand people; it is one of the liveliest venues in the city.

There are a couple of reinforced glass portals in the floors which display the old wells that lead to a secret underground lake; its supply of water was the reason the brewery was established here.

An underground freshwater lake was the perfect excuse to create Cains Brewery Village above it.

LIVERPOOL
(Cavern Quarter to Docks)

Starting at the edge of the Cavern Quarter, the route loops around the back of the conservation area at the top of the Georgian Quarter, before heading into the heart of Beatles territory.

Emerging at Royal Albert Dock, it follows the water's edge through one of the UK's most popular tourist areas, before heading back into the south of the city.

I absolutely adore the mix of pubs along this route, and while my favourites are the Baltic Fleet and the Bridewell, it is impossible to ignore just how special the iconic Cavern Club is.

The route is essential for any traveller looking to immerse themselves in the area's rich musical history while also observing the impact of the explosive growth and rapid development of this major industrial centre.

Start at Moorfields station (L2 2BS).

1. **Ye Hole in Ye Wall** *1.00 p.m.*
   4 Hackins Hey, L2 2AW

2. **The Lion Tavern** *1.30 p.m.*
   67 Moorfields, L2 2BP

3. **Shenanigans** *2.15 p.m.*
   77 Tithebarn Street, L2 2EN

4. **The Ship & Mitre** *3.00 p.m.*
   133 Dale Street, L2 2JH

5. **White Star** *3.30 p.m.*
   2–4 Rainford Gardens, L2 6PT

6. **The Grapes** *4.15 p.m.*
   25 Mathew Street, L2 6RE

7. **The Cavern Club (£5 entry fee)** *4.45 p.m.*
   10 Mathew Street, L2 6RE

8. **The Old Bank** *5.30 p.m.*
   James Street, L2 7NE

9. **Pump House** *6.30 p.m.*
   Albert Dock, L3 4AN

10. **Baltic Fleet** *7.15 p.m.*
    33A Wapping, L1 8DQ

11. **The Bridewell** *8.00 p.m.*
    1 Campbell Square, L1 5FB

12. **The Monro** *9.00 p.m.*
    Duke Street, L1 5AG

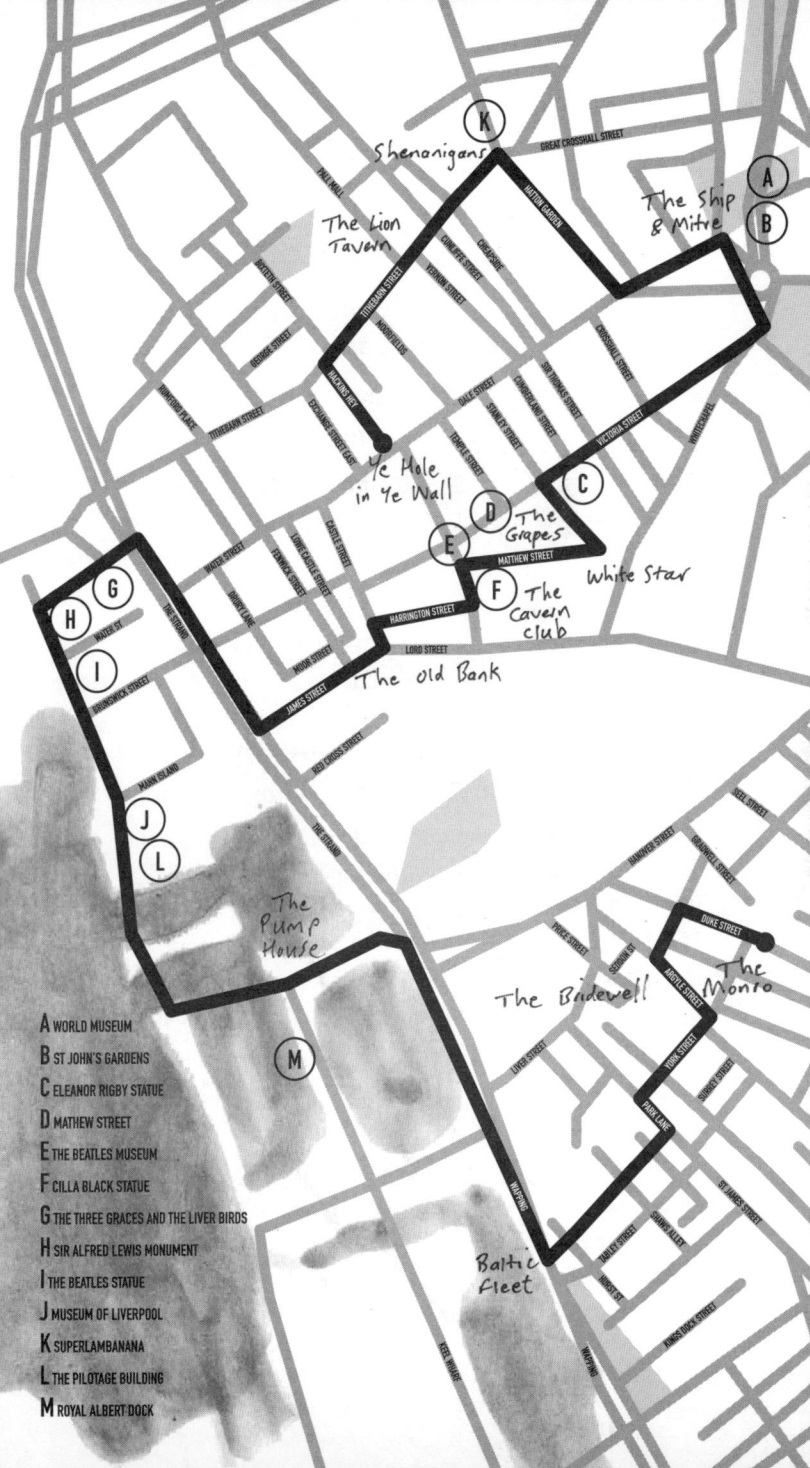

A WORLD MUSEUM
B ST JOHN'S GARDENS
C ELEANOR RIGBY STATUE
D MATHEW STREET
E THE BEATLES MUSEUM
F CILLA BLACK STATUE
G THE THREE GRACES AND THE LIVER BIRDS
H SIR ALFRED LEWIS MONUMENT
I THE BEATLES STATUE
J MUSEUM OF LIVERPOOL
K SUPERLAMBANANA
L THE PILOTAGE BUILDING
M ROYAL ALBERT DOCK

DIRECTIONS

Leave Moorfields station and turn left, then right onto Dale Street where **Ye Hole in Ye Wall (1)** is a couple of blocks along down Hackins Hey. Continue past the pub and turn right at the end of the road to **The Lion Tavern (2)** on the corner of the next big road. Further along, on the opposite side, is **Shenanigans (3)**.

Go back along the main road to the junction, before turning right down Hatton Garden, and as the road curves left **The Ship & Mitre (4)** is on the corner.

Follow the road past the pub, as it curves right on the busy junction behind the World Museum **(A)** and St John's Gardens **(B)** before walking along Victoria Street and turning left on Stanley Street. Head past Eleanor Rigby **(C)**, taking a first right onto Mathew Street where the **White Star (5)** is a few doors down the first left. Head back to turn left at Mathew Street **(D)** to **The Grapes (6)** and then continue past the Beatles Museum **(E)** and the Cilla Black Statue **(F)** on to **The Cavern Club (7)**. Turn left at the end of the road and then take the first right, before turning on Castle Street and following the road as it curves right to **The Old Bank (8)** on the corner. Past the pub, turn right on the main road, before crossing the road past the Liver Building **(G, H)** and then heading back along the water's edge past the Beatles statue **(I)**, the Museum of Liverpool **(J)** the SuperLambanana **(K)** and the Pilotage Building **(L)**, before turning left alongside Canning Dock to **The Pump House (9, M)**. Head straight out of the pub, between the docks, turn left at the end, and then head right along the main road where **Baltic Fleet (10)** is on the corner. Head along Cornhill and turn left at the end of the road, before taking the first right and heading left once past the small pedestrian area, and turn left where **The Bridewell (11)** is over the road opposite Seddon Street. Follow the parallel pedestrian area along Campbell Street before emerging at Duke Street and turning right to **The Monro (12)**, which is on the next block.

---

1. YE HOLE IN YE WALL

Built in 1726, this is rumoured to be the oldest pub in the city. It was built on the site of an old Quaker cemetery, which has resulted in the cellar being located on the first floor, above the bar.

Staff have often noticed ghostly goings-on, with the legend of at least two spirits: the first a hooded figure of unknown origin, and the second an eighteenth-century Spanish sailor who was stabbed in the pub for not accepting the King's shilling.

Until 1977, this pub did not admit women, making it one of the last men-only pubs in the city.

It is said that Adolf Hitler was a frequent customer during visits to his sister who was studying in the city.

2. THE LION TAVERN

Getting its name from the Lion locomotive that was present on the Liverpool to Manchester railway lines, it's thought to have gained its licence around 1840.

The eponymous locomotive can be found in the Museum of Liverpool, and has been there since it opened in 2010.

The original pub was extended in 1915 by its owner, Cains brewery, with the installation of Art Nouveau tiling, stained glass, an ornate woodworked bar and cut-glass windows.

Although no longer functioning, the original brass bells used by customers to attract the attention of the bar staff remain in place above the seats in both lounges of the pub.

3. SHENANIGANS

One of Liverpool's seven original streets, Tithebarn Street (formerly Moor Street), takes its name from the tithe barn built by Lord Molyneux in 1524 on this site.

By 1820 the barn had gone and, to accommodate the explosion in the city's population during the Industrial Revolution, the street was widened. Just over twenty years later there were eighteen licensed premises on the road; 'beer vaults' became a common sight.

It was around this time that the first evidence of this pub

appeared under the licence of Hugh Skellern, although its name is unknown before 1860, when it was called the Spirit Vaults; by 1894 it was the Revolving Lamp. Later it was taken over and renamed Walker's by Peter Walker and his son.

One of the few buildings in the area to survive bombing in World War II, it became Shenanigans in 1997 when it was opened by three brothers, the McDonalds, who had moved to the city from Ireland.

It's also been a popular destination for social media influencers with several, such as 'The Guinness Guru', naming it the city's best pint.

4. THE SHIP & MITRE

This pub in an Art Deco building got its name from its two previous incarnations – the Flagship and the Mitre.

It is believed to have been the site of a coach house until the current building was constructed in 1935 – with several extensive renovations in the downstairs bar creating the illusion of being inside a ship.

A. WORLD MUSEUM

Originally the 'Derby Museum' as it contained the 13th Earl of Derby's natural history collection when it opened in 1851; it also used to share the premises with a library.

Public demand meant that it quickly outgrew the premises and a new purpose-built museum was opened in 1860.

Expansion and refurbishment continued, despite suffering damage during the Blitz in World War II, and, since being renamed in 2005, it has featured a variety of exhibitions including a planetarium, Egyptian antiquities, botany and a time tunnel showing changing geology over time.

B. ST JOHN'S GARDENS

This large open space is part of the William Brown Street conservation area; with its distinctive public buildings it is often referred to as Liverpool's 'cultural quarter'.

It has been the location of several different types of buildings over time, and as far back as 1749 the city's first general infirmary was constructed on the site – before a seamen's hospital, a dispensary and then a 'lunatic asylum' followed over the next forty years.

The sloped land and exposed location made it perfect for windmills and public washing lines, and the land was also used as a public cemetery until it reached capacity in 1854 and the bodies were moved; the adjoining church was demolished at the end of the nineteenth century.

C. ELEANOR RIGBY STATUE

The seated bronze figure, representing the subject of the eponymous Beatles song, was unveiled in December 1982.

It was created by popular entertainer Tommy Steele, who was performing in Liverpool at the time.

The costs for the figure were largely covered by the council and the *Echo* newspaper, and it has several objects inside it, representing good luck (a four-leafed clover), spiritual guidance (a bible), sport and fun (football boots), comedy and adventure (a comic book), and love (a sonnet). Ultimately, the statue implies more hope than the song it is named after, which ends with the eponymous Eleanor Rigby dying alone with nobody to attend her funeral.

Sometimes a bench is a welcome resting point between pubs.

5. WHITE STAR

Named after the shipping company of *Titanic* fame, this 1880 pub was where the Beatles were believed to have been paid for their early gigs by managers Bob Wooler and Alan Williams.

Alongside shipping-liner memorabilia and images, the back room is adorned with tributes to the Beatles – known as the Beatles Back Wall.

The shipping company, founded in Liverpool in 1845, was one of the most prominent in the world, and focused on passenger comfort over speed.

It is well remembered for the loss of several notable passenger liners, most famously the *Titanic* in 1912, but also the *Atlantic* (1873), the *Republic* (1909) and the *Britannic* (1916).

It fell into decline during the Great Depression and merged with the Cunard Line, its main rival, in 1934.

D. MATHEW STREET

This popular tourist destination is surrounded by attractions and several pubs linked to the Beatles, making it one of the most popular nightlife destinations in the city.

Its unusual spelling of the name comes from a notable merchant, Mathew Pluckington, in whose time the area was predominantly a fruit and vegetable market.

The street features several monuments and statues, including one of Swiss psychiatrist Carl Jung, who shared a dream he had about the city in his autobiography.

6. THE GRAPES

One of the Beatles' favourite venues, it was built in 1804, making it one of the city's oldest, and up until the 1960s it was one of the only pubs on the famous street, among the warehouses.

On my last visit the pub claimed to have a Banksy, however I couldn't confirm and let the truth get in the way of a good story!

E. THE BEATLES MUSEUM

This distinctive five-storey building showcases more than three hundred items – from a total collection of 1,200 since its opening in 2018.

It features memorabilia such as George Harrison's first guitar, John Lennon's medals from *Sergeant Pepper* and his custom 'egg' chair, and Paul McCartney's bass speaker.

F. CILLA BLACK STATUE

The statue was erected in 2017, just two years after the entertainer's death A proud Liverpudlian, Cilla honoured her home town in her song 'Liverpool Lullaby'.

Active in show business for more than fifty years, her big break came as her friends the Beatles championed her to further success when her first two singles reached number one in the UK charts.

Following the success of her music career she moved to television presenting, hosting light entertainment shows *Blind Date* and *Surprise Surprise*.

Her stage name was due to a mistake in the *Mersey Beat* paper, when publisher Bill Harry mixed up the colour in her real name – Priscilla White.

7. THE CAVERN CLUB

Opened in 1957, originally as a jazz club, it became the heart of Liverpool's rock and roll scene in the late 1950s and early 1960s, and is most fondly linked to the Beatles and the Merseybeat style that also saw the emergence of Gerry and the Pacemakers, the Searchers and Cilla Black.

The venue was originally a fruit warehouse, with the cellar having been used as an air-raid shelter during World War II. In warm weather the heat from dancers in the packed venue would cause the bricks to 'sweat' the scent from the stored fruit, creating the colloquially named 'Cavern Perfume' on revellers.

Despite the success of skiffle groups, John Lennon's first band – the Quarrymen – were booked and, after an argument about the set list, went on to perform Elvis's 'Don't Be Cruel'.

Despite the ensuing kerfuffle the band returned and played with Paul McCartney for the first time in January 1958.

The Beatles' first official appearance at the club was on 9 February 1961, after they had returned from Hamburg.

Over the next two years they went on to make 292 appearances at the club, with the last one concluding just six months before their first trip to the US in 1964 and at the onset of 'Beatlemania'.

The period also saw performances from the likes of the Rolling Stones, the Yardbirds, the Hollies, the Kinks, Elton John, Queen, the Who and many more. Many acts performed while Cilla Black worked in the cloakroom before her own climb to stardom.

The original club closed in 1973, with a replacement opening shortly after.

Plans in 1981 led to the development of the area and the attempted excavation of the original club, but the old cellar's structure had been too badly damaged by the demolition of the warehouses above it.

The remodelled replacement now sits at a 90-degree angle to the original and covers more than two-thirds of its original footprint, with the 'Live Lounge' being an exact replica of the original; its construction used many of the old, excavated bricks.

The fire exit, adjacent to the Cilla Black statue, is the original entrance.

Several replicas and tributes to the famous music venue have sprung up across the world, including in the USA, Argentina, New Zealand, Tokyo, Australia and Lanzarote.

On my last visit, I had to pinch myself as I sat with my pint in the dressing room that has hosted some of the most famous musical names on the planet, before taking that walk to the stage (although there was no one there to see me).

One of the most famous music venues in the world, it was here that the Beatles found their fame.

8. THE OLD BANK

Initially a branch of the First National Bank, it was constructed in 1920 and was relaunched as a pub in 2018, with seating installed on the former banking room floor, drinking areas occupying the mezzanine floor and the creation of an island bar.

By the famous statue, under the gaze of the Liver Birds, Ben has shared most of these routes as my trusted cameraman as we've captured the journey for my social media.

G. THE THREE GRACES AND THE LIVER BIRDS

Built on the site of the former George's Dock, the Three Graces are waterside buildings: the Royal Liver Building (completed in 1911), the Cunard Building (the former headquarters of the eponymous shipping company, completed in 1917) and the Port of Liverpool Building (the former Mersey Docks and Harbour board headquarters, completed in 1907).

The most iconic of the three, the Liver Building, was the home of the Royal Liver Association, which operated from 1850 to 2011, to provide shared financial support after the death of the household earner, which in its early days was most often the husband/father.

The building was one of the UK's first to be constructed using reinforced concrete and is grade I listed. It is recognisable for the liver bird sculptures atop each of its two clock towers, watching over the city from a spot that was once among the tallest buildings in the country.

Resembling the cormorant, the liver is a mythical bird that was first depicted as a generic bird, with a sprig of plant in its beak, on the city's seal dating from 1352.

Although probably intended to be a more regal eagle, the poor draughtsmanship and subsequent adaptations have left the birds' real identity somewhat of a mystery.

While the liver bird is indelibly linked to Liverpool Football Club, and has been the club's mascot since 2012, the first club to use it as a symbol was the other Merseyside club, Everton.

H. SIR ALFRED LEWIS MONUMENT

This tribute to the Welsh ship owner was erected in 1913 and is ornately decorated with a liver bird, a crown and a tabard.

Lewis was a major figure of the colonial shipping trade and is credited with introducing the banana to the UK. His fleet numbered more than a hundred ships at the time of his death and he was described by newspaper editor W. T. Stead as the 'Uncrowned King of West Africa'.

I. THE BEATLES STATUE

The four bronze figures, installed by Andy Edwards in 2015, seen strolling through Pier Head, are larger than real life and are based on a 1963 photo of the 'Fab Four' taken at this location.

McCartney is seen holding a camera, as a tribute to his late wife Linda; Ringo's right shoe features the L8 postcode where he grew up; Harrison's belt includes a Sanskrit inscription due to his following of Hare Krishna tradition; and Lennon's right hand holds two acorns cast from some collected from trees near the location of his death, and represent him mailing acorns to world leaders as a message of peace in the 1960s.

J. MUSEUM OF LIVERPOOL

This modern addition to the city's museums was opened in 2011, and went on to host the G7 summit ten years later.

It focuses on the city's history as a port and how the Industrial Revolution and British Empire impacted the economic development of the area.

K. SUPERLAMBANANA

The first sculpture was bright yellow, stood over 16 feet tall and was a cross between a lamb and a banana. Created by four local artists, it was a replica of a design by NYC based Japanese artist Taro Chiezo.

The sculpture was always intended to move around the city, having started near the Liver Building, and although it was only initially on loan, a replica was made in 2008 – with a further 125 miniature versions scattered across the city – for a European Capital of Culture event before finding a permanent home next to the Museum of Liverpool.

L. THE PILOTAGE BUILDING

Opened in 1883 as the headquarters of the Liverpool Pilot's Office, it was operational until 1978, although the service to help ships navigate the River Mersey had been operational since 1766.

9. THE PUMP HOUSE

Part of the fashionable Albert Dock area, this modern pub opened in 1984; it was originally built in 1870 as a world-first hydraulic pumping system which supplied power to the historic dockyard.

On a sunny day, the beer garden is one of the best places to sit in the city, overlooking the still waters of the docks and the iconic area that used to have UNESCO World Heritage status.

Despite the arctic conditions the view over the Albert Dock is a serene sight.

M. ROYAL ALBERT DOCK

Granted its honorific name in 2018, the large complex of dock buildings was opening 1846 and was the first structure in Britain not to use any structural wood.

Its innovative design enabled the unloading and loading of ships directly into (or from) the warehouses. However, with the influx of tea, cotton, silks, tobacco, brandy and sugar, among many more products from around the world, the volume of shipments quickly outgrew the dock and it shifted to become a more common storage site.

In modern times it has become the most visited multi-use tourist attraction in the UK outside of London, being home to several museums, monuments and art galleries.

Whenever you visit you will find a massive anchor in the docks!

10. BALTIC FLEET

This 1850s flatiron pub is decorated with a nautical theme and originally had many external doors, allowing patrons to escape press gangs (groups that would forcibly conscript men into the military or the navy).

The extra doors ensured that there was rarely a punch-up inside the pub – although most runners exited the pub into the arms of their captors.

There are rumours that the cellars contain tunnels leading to the dock to enable smugglers, and into the red-light district of Cornhill so that sailors could satisfy their lust with sex workers after a long time at sea.

It's got a great reputation for serving ales and craft beer, and on my last visit the owner, Simon, had the fires going and showed us the cellars and the coal holes – we didn't find any secret tunnels.

11. THE BRIDEWELL

As the name suggests, this was originally a bridewell – a type of prison or reform school for petty offenders.

The prison and adjoining fire station were built in the 1840s and the seven cells were usually occupied by overexuberant sailors and dockers – with about a hundred locked up each month.

In 1860, Charles Dickens was sworn in for the night while researching his collection of writings, *The Uncommercial Traveller*.

Although it ceased to be a prison in 1932, it was rumoured to have been used by the US military in World War II for conscientious objectors and German prisoners of war.

The band Frankie Goes to Hollywood was formed here in 1982 when the then derelict building was brought back to life as a rehearsal space for local bands; most of *Welcome to the Pleasuredome* was written here.

12. THE MONRO

This distinctive grade II listed Georgian former merchant's house was constructed in 1746 and was one of the first buildings on the street.

Its name comes from the first passenger ship that travelled to New York in 1817.

Be careful upstairs, as one of the rooms has had its damaged floor removed to create a feature that enables you to peer down onto the busy bar below.

Producing pub crawls has led me to star with Robbie and Dan on their famous Moon Under the Water *podcast, where we named my future pub 'The Crawlers Rest'.*

NOTTINGHAM
(Castle to City)

Coming in strong as a contender for the home of the UK's oldest pub, Nottingham has three pubs that may fit the bill. Our route starts at the canal before passing the famous castle, winding through the market square and ending up at one of the most spectacular locations in the country for a pub.

A variety of local micro breweries keep the city's many pubs well stocked with a huge range of beers.

What I love about this route is that, although Nottingham is a city, everywhere feels close and walkable. Much of the centre is connected through a series of caves and tunnels, many of which have been converted into pub cellars over the years, keeping the beer, lager, stouts and ciders cool. Several local establishments will even accommodate a brief viewing.

The Trip is one of the best pubs I've ever visited and a definite highlight of the route.

Start from Nottingham station (NG2 3AQ).

1. **The Canalhouse** *1.00 p.m.*
48–52 Canal Street, NG1 7EH

2. **Ye Olde Trip to Jerusalem** *1.45 p.m.*
Brewhouse Yard, NG1 6AD

3. **The Castle** *2.30 p.m.*
1 Castle Road, NG1 6AA

4. **Ye Olde Salutation Inn** *3.00 p.m.*
Hounds Gate, NG1 7AA

5. **Malt Cross** *3.45 p.m.*
16 St James's Street, NG1 6FG

6. **The Bell Inn** *4.30 p.m.*
18 Angel Row, NG1 6HL

7. **Pit & Pendulum** *5.30 p.m.*
17 Victoria Street, NG1 2EW

8. **The Kilpin Beer Cafe** *6.30 p.m.*
10 Bridlesmith Walk, NG1 2HB

9. **Kean's Head** *7.30 p.m.*
46 St Mary's Gate, NG1 1QA

10. **Pitcher & Piano** *8.30 p.m.*
High Pavement, NG1 1HN

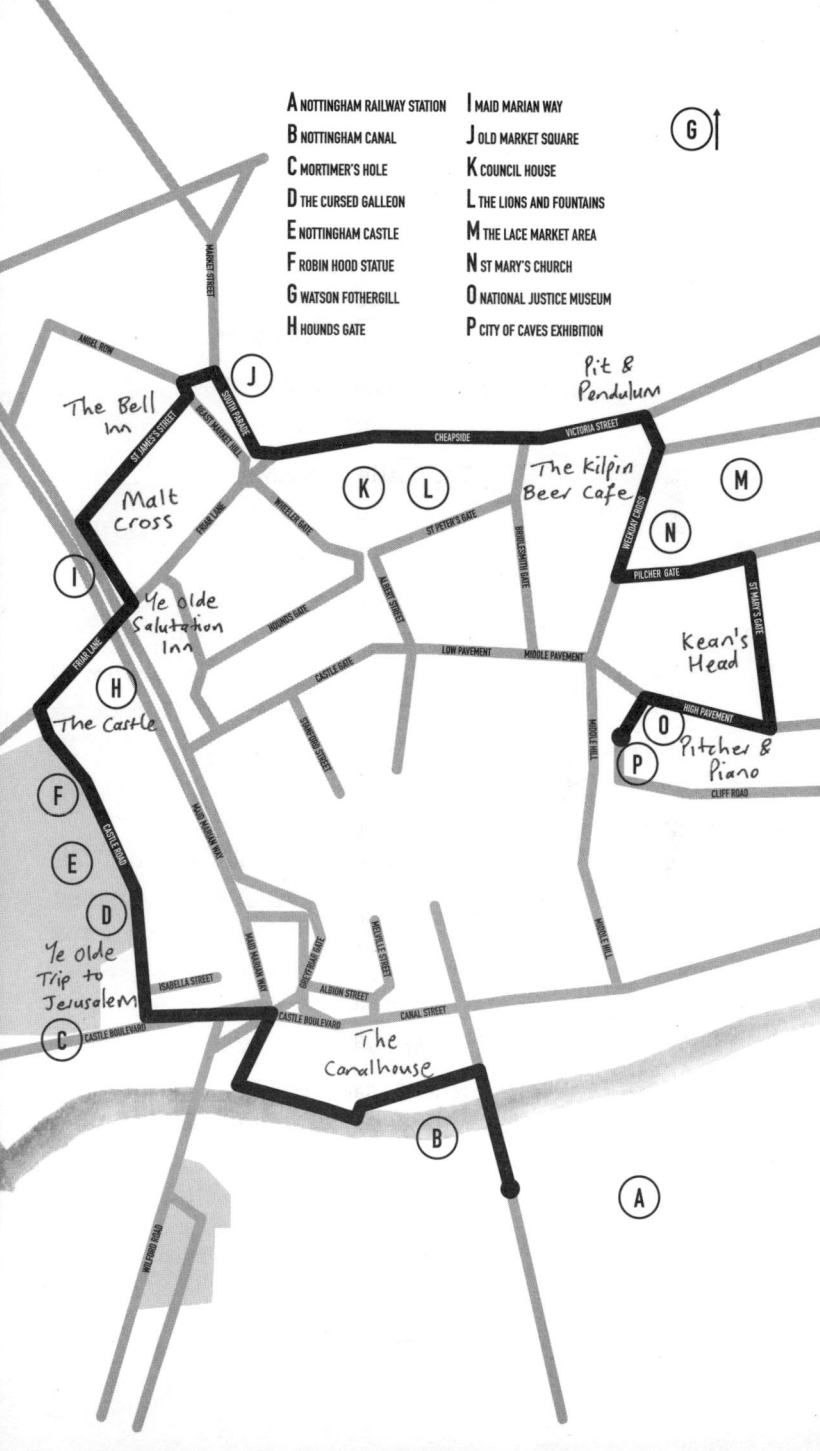

A NOTTINGHAM RAILWAY STATION
B NOTTINGHAM CANAL
C MORTIMER'S HOLE
D THE CURSED GALLEON
E NOTTINGHAM CASTLE
F ROBIN HOOD STATUE
G WATSON FOTHERGILL
H HOUNDS GATE

I MAID MARIAN WAY
J OLD MARKET SQUARE
K COUNCIL HOUSE
L THE LIONS AND FOUNTAINS
M THE LACE MARKET AREA
N ST MARY'S CHURCH
O NATIONAL JUSTICE MUSEUM
P CITY OF CAVES EXHIBITION

The Bell Inn
Malt Cross
Ye olde Salutation Inn
The Castle
Ye Olde Trip to Jerusalem

Pit & Pendulum
The Kilpin Beer Cafe
Kean's Head
Pitcher & Piano

The Canalhouse

ANGEL ROW
MARKET STREET
ST JAMES'S STREET
SOUTH PARADE
ST AND MARKET HILL
FLETCHER GATE
WHEELER GATE
CHEAPSIDE
VICTORIA STREET
ST PETER'S GATE
BROAD SMITH GATE
WEEKDAY CROSS
PILCHER GATE
ST MARY'S GATE
ALBERT STREET
FRIAR LANE
HOUNDS GATE
LOW PAVEMENT
MIDDLE PAVEMENT
CASTLE GATE
HIGH PAVEMENT
STANFORD STREET
MIDDLE HILL
MIDDLE PAVEMENT
CLIFF ROAD
MAID MARIAN WAY
CASTLE ROAD
ISABELLA STREET
CASTLE BOULEVARD
GREYFRIAR GATE
MIDDLE STREET
ALBION STREET
CANAL STREET
WILFORD ROAD

DIRECTIONS

Exit the station **(A)** and turn right, heading over the canal **(B)** before turning left at the junction where **The Canalhouse (1)** is on the left. Turn left from the pub and continue along the main road, crossing at the first major junction **(C)** where **Ye Olde Trip to Jerusalem (2, D)** is down Castle Road, the first right.

Exit the pub to the left and follow the walls of the castle **(E, F)** to the main entrance where **The Castle (3, G)** is opposite. Follow Hounds Gate **(H)** alongside the pub and cross over Maid Marian Way where **Ye Olde Salutation Inn (4)** is on the other side of the road.

Turn right when leaving the side of the pub against the main road **(I)**, and continue to St James's Street on the right where, about halfway down, is **The Malt Cross (5)** and at the end of the road, to the left, is **The Bell Inn (6)**.

Leave the pub and head through the square **(J)**, passing the Council House **(K, L)** on the right-hand side, where just past this on the left is **The Pit & Pendulum (7)**.

Follow the road as it curves right, and look out for Bridle-smith Walk, a tiny alleyway opposite the car park which is easy to miss, but it hides **The Kilpin Beer Cafe (8)**. After heading back to the main road, follow Pilcher Gate **(M)** on the opposite side of the road, over the narrow paved area before turning right down to **Kean's Head (9)** opposite Saint Mary's Church **(N)**.

Past the pub, turn right at the end of the road past the National Justice Museum **(O)** where **Pitcher & Piano (10)** is just before the City of Caves **(P)** attraction.

A. NOTTINGHAM RAILWAY STATION

The second busiest station in the Midlands after Birmingham New Street, Nottingham railway station was opened in 1848 before being rebuilt in 1904. This occurred shortly after Great Central Railway's opening of nearby Nottingham Victoria station.

The rebuilding was ordered quickly as the original station had become cramped, with more than 170 staff working across only three platforms.

In 1896, a light engine collided with six empty fish trucks, resulting in the trucks being thrown from the tracks onto the supporting columns. This caused a portion of the roof to collapse, injuring six people.

The remodelled station was built in an Edwardian baroque revival style but was opened in a state of chaos as the (now nine) platforms were not expected to be ready for several months.

On the morning of 12 January 2018, the station was severely damaged when a fire started in the women's toilet in the newly built section of the station. Ten fire engines and fifty firefighters from Nottingham and Derbyshire battled the blaze.

The fire was treated as arson and in August 2019, a thirty-four-year-old woman received a two-year jail sentence, having admitted to accidentally setting fire to a bin while using heroin and crack. The repair reportedly cost around £5.6 million.

B. NOTTINGHAM CANAL

Connecting to the River Trent, this 14.7-mile stretch of canal was constructed to bypass a difficult-to-manoeuvre section around Trent Bridge.

It opened in 1796 and saw a continual increase in traffic until 1804. Around this time, competition from the railways threatened waterway transport, and ultimately it was the trains that lasted the test of time. In the 1840s, a real decline in use occurred. It passed through the hands of several companies and managers, but commercial operations ceased in 1937.

1. THE CANALHOUSE

Built as a canal-side warehouse in 1895, it was repurposed to a canal museum in the 1980s, just under a hundred years later.

Now a grade II listed building, the adjacent canal runs into the pub, and there are narrowboats moored inside.

Most of the times I have been here, the sun has been shining and the waterside garden is heaving with hen parties and stag dos on their way into the city centre – but don't let that put you off, as they very rarely turn left and head towards the castle.

C. MORTIMER'S HOLE

This long passage, cut into the rock, leads from Brewhouse Yard into the castle mansion over 127 steps and is often open for tours.

Legend has it that the passage was used to capture the medieval queen Isabella (known as the She-Wolf of France) and her lover, Roger Mortimer.

2. YE OLDE TRIP TO JERUSALEM

A contender for one of England's oldest pubs, the Trip claims to have been established in 1189 when it was named after King Richard the Lionheart's third crusade to the Holy Land. It has changed hands and locations many times since then, so authentication is a challenge.

The pub is built into the castle walls and, although the oldest parts of the current building date back to around 1650, there is evidence that the caves were used as a castle brewhouse as early as 1067.

The current cellars were converted from an old jailhouse that used to hold the condemned before they were led to the gallows at the corner of the castle.

Upstairs, the museum room contains medieval ornaments and a tapestry depicting the history of Nottingham.

I was lucky when I visited, as the landlord, Karl, was eager to share behind-the-scenes access and we explored the cellars and the winding, narrow tunnels that are closed to the public.

D. THE CURSED GALLEON

Encased in glass, this dusty ornament above the Rock Bar on the first floor of the Trip was sealed after several people who had cleaned it, mysteriously, and suddenly, passed away.

E. NOTTINGHAM CASTLE

An important royal fortress throughout the years, it dates back as far as 1068, when it was the site of a wooden motte-and-bailey Norman castle.

Its location, at a vital crossing of the River Trent, made the castle one of the most strategically important for military and royalty.

Due to its proximity to Sherwood Forest, noblemen would come for the popular pastime of hunting, spending their days collecting game animals for servants to prepare into lavish dinners.

During Richard the Lionheart's absence while he was fighting in the Crusades, the castle was occupied by the Sheriff of Nottingham and other supporters of Prince John – this is now widely known from the legend and tales of Robin Hood.

After it was recaptured, it remained an important royal residence for centuries until the outbreak of the English Civil War, when much of the original castle was demolished following an artillery battering during the mid-seventeenth century.

The Restoration-style mansion built in 1660 sits on 'Castle Rock', with its 130-foot cliffs dominating the city skyline.

By 1875 the buildings had become little more than a derelict shell and restoration work commenced, leading to its opening in 1878 as the Nottingham Castle Museum.

F. ROBIN HOOD STATUE

Installed in 1952, it represents the legendary, heroic outlaw who is depicted in English folklore.

He first appeared around the thirteenth century, in tales of a legendary archer and swordsman said to steal from the rich to give to the poor. There is still much scholarly debate about how true the stories are, and if Robin Hood existed at all.

The earliest historical records, from 1226, mention a man named Robert Hod having thirty-two shillings confiscated before he went on to become an outlaw. The outlaw Roger Godberd, a supporter of Simon de Montfort from the mid-thirteenth century, has also been mentioned as the possible true inspiration for Robin Hood. De Montfort was the 6th Earl of Leicester, and led a rebellion against the rule of King Henry III, later known as the Second Barons' War.

There are many interpretations of the character: he is sometimes described as a nobleman or having fought in the Crusades. Over the years certain details of the myth have consolidated around Robin Hood, including an extended group of characters, including Maid Marian, Little John, Friar Tuck and Alan-a-Dale.

By the early fifteenth century, the character had become associated with May Day celebrations, with revellers dressed in his distinctive Lincoln green outfit. There have been many movies and TV shows based on Robin Hood, including a Disney animation in 1973 in which he was depicted as a fox.

Although there are many theories on the real identity of Robin Hood, it has been suggested that the name was used as an alias by all thieves and outlaws in the area.

3. THE CASTLE

This 1883 building was designed and built in the unique style of Watson Fothergill, whose Gothic revival can be seen in more than a hundred Nottingham buildings.

The grade II listed pub sits opposite the castle entrance and the famous, historic gatehouse.

You'll never guess who I bumped into outside of The Castle . . . only Robin Hood ready to strike with his bow and arrow!

G. WATSON FOTHERGILL

Fothergill was a prolific architect who mixed Gothic revival and English vernacular styles in more than a hundred buildings throughout Nottingham, including his office on George Street, the Woodborough Road Baptist Chapel, Queen's Chambers and the Black Boy Hotel at Long Row.

His earliest known surviving building dates to 1866, two years after he set up his practice, which was active until around 1912.

H. HOUNDS GATE

First referenced in 1326, when it was named as Hungate, this historic street is believed to get its name from being the location for the kennels of the nearby castle. Dogs played a big role in medieval society, joining nobility on hunts and being the first protection many houses had against intruders.

There are several notable buildings along the street. These were predominantly built around 1900, as for much of the street's history it was badly built and maintained. In 1808, the inhabitants of the parish of St Nicholas paid to have the street repaired, leading to a more prosperous future.

4. YE OLDE SALUTATION INN

Once claimed to be the most haunted pub in England, with an impressive eighty-nine resident ghosts, this seventeenth-century pub sits on a labyrinth of caves from the ninth century. They were originally used as the storerooms for a Saxon farm.

Although much of the city is built on caves, these are unusually large, with two levels and a well shaft sunk nearly 80 feet into the rock.

Over time the caves have seen many uses: King Edward III's secret meeting room, the location where Oliver Cromwell is said to have signed King Charles I's death warrant, and home to a colony of lepers.

Affectionately nicknamed the Sal, parts of the building are believed to date back to 1240.

Rumours that Dick Turpin was nearly apprehended at the pub have never been confirmed.

I. MAID MARIAN WAY

The heroine of the Robin Hood tales and sometimes interpreted as his lover, she does not appear in the tales until the 1600s.

She is generally portrayed as a strong female character, celebrated for her bravery and independence as an important member of Robin's inner circle.

5. THE MALT CROSS

Taking its name from a monument that used to be in the market square, this 1877 building is one of the few Victorian music halls still standing.

Its construction is distinctive due to a high-arched glazed roof held up by wooden arches built from layers of laminated wood bent to the required curve and held together by glue. This technique bypassed the usual difficulties of wooden arch design, and the layers left no visible nail or bolt holes.

As we film all the pubs in the book for social media, we've managed to capture me hitting over a hundred 180s – with a little editing finesse of course.

J. OLD MARKET SQUARE

Located in the heart of the city, it is one of the largest paved squares in the UK and covers approximately 3 acres.

Built when Nottingham was a Norman town known as Snothryngham or Snottingham, the square formed the centre point for market trade, large gatherings and events.

It was as large as 5.5 acres from the eleventh century, until in 1928 when the seven-hundred-year-old Goose Fair was moved to another location. It was decided some of the space would be better used as a residential area and the square was redeveloped alongside the construction of the Council House.

Locals have affectionately nicknamed the spaced 'Slab Square' after the granite slabs installed during the 2007 re-design. The city's coat of arms was renovated and reinstalled near the Royal Concert Hall entrance around the same time.

As well as being a focal point for celebrating sporting victories, such as Nottingham Forest's European Cup victory parade and Torvill and Dean's Olympic gold medal, the square has been a focal point for significant moments like the Luddites' protest and rioting against the 1831 Second Reform Bill.

The 'speakers' corner' is the first official location of its kind outside of London and was opened in 2009 by the then justice secretary, Jack Straw. A speakers' corner is an area in a city centre designated as a place where public speaking, debate and discussion are allowed.

6. THE BELL INN

There has been a friary guesthouse on the site of this pub since before 1271, and this pub is claimed to be one of the country's oldest.

Carbon dating of the timbers indicates that the current building was constructed in 1420, before becoming an alehouse in 1539.

The first record in which it was mentioned came in 1638, in the will of freeholder John White. In more recent times, it celebrated a hundred years of ownership by the Jackson family in 2013.

Among its notable features are leprosy windows to the right of the entrance, where patrons had to show they had the correct number of fingers before they were allowed to enter.

The Long Room features original wallpaper, timber crown-posts and wooden beams from 1437.

The extensive cave network of cellars underneath the pub is open to the public for guided tours and includes the original cock-fighting pit and a well that can be seen from the end of the main bar.

I enjoy meeting new people along the route, such as Dale and Holly, of Great British Pub Crawl fame, outside Nottingham Castle.

K. COUNCIL HOUSE

The de facto centre of the city is marked by the impressive 200-foot dome on this grade II* listed building, which was completed in 1929.

Formerly the headquarters of Nottingham City Council, it is now used as an upmarket shopping parade called The Exchange, and most council administrative services have been moved to nearby Loxley House.

The neo-baroque building houses 'Little John' within its belfry – weighing over 10 tons, it is the deepest-toned clock bell in the UK and can be heard from up to seven miles away. It got its name from the companion of Robin Hood, who was also called little while actually being rather large.

Throughout the interior of the building are elaborate decorations and architecture, with a grand marble staircase sweeping to the first floor, where there is a ballroom inspired by the Palace of Versailles, the Lord Mayor's Suite, an elegant tea room and the council's chambers.

L. THE LIONS AND FOUNTAINS

Two large stone lions named Agamemnon and Menelaus guard the Council House steps. They were sculpted by Joseph Else, the principal of the Nottingham School of Art, between 1923 and 1939.

Despite the reference to Greek mythology, they are more affectionately known as Leon and Oscar, or Lennie and Ronnie.

At the square's completion in 1929, the edges were adorned with grass and flowers. However, they were cleared and filled with water at the onset of World War II, to provide reserves for local firefighters to use during German bombing raids.

7. THE PIT & PENDULUM

The pub's name is taken from the title of an 1842 short story by American writer Edgar Allan Poe, in which he details the torment of a victim of the Spanish Inquisition.

The eerie, gothic theme continues throughout the pub, and the toilets are notoriously difficult to find.

This gothic pub does a great job of confusing customers by hiding the toilets behind a bookcase.

M. THE LACE MARKET AREA

Once the centre-point of the world's lace industry, the area is sited on the original Saxon settlement, and the nineteenth-century industrial architecture has resulted in the location being granted protected heritage status.

More than 25,000 – mostly female – workers powered the hosiery industry at its peak in the 1890s, and although the area did not include a trading market, it was densely packed with salesrooms and warehouses.

By the 1970s the working population had shrunk to fewer than five thousand as technology advances had left many of the factories derelict and the area falling into decline.

8. THE KILPIN BEER CAFE

This hidden pub on the edge of the lace market area was a restaurant until it was converted in 2016.

It is named after football pioneer Herbert Kilpin, a lace worker who followed his trade to Italy in 1890. After his employer, Edoardo Bosio, founded Internazionale Torino as the first official Italian football team, he became the first Englishman to play abroad.

In 1898, after moving to Milan, Kilpin was one of the founding members of the 'Milan Foot-Ball and Cricket Club' who would win the league title in just their second season and go on to become the esteemed AC Milan.

After nine seasons at the club, he remained working in Milan and, although very little is documented about his life, he died aged forty-six, in 1916.

The pub's interior is interesting as it is split across several levels with a small bar, run by a friendly team; it also shares a garden with its neighbour.

9. KEAN'S HEAD

The current grade II listed building, opposite St Mary's Church, was constructed in 1907 as a warehouse and office space, on the site of a nineteenth-century pub.

The original pub was connected to actor Edmund Kean who appeared as Hamlet at the nearby Old Theatre Royal, which was built around 1760. When it closed in 1837, the theatre was transformed almost immediately into a music hall.

The current taproom adopts the name of the original. It opened in 2004 and was the first non-smoking pub in Nottingham.

N. ST MARY'S CHURCH

At the heart of the lace market area, this grade I listed church was mentioned in the 1086 Domesday Book.

Parts of the building date back to 1377. The chantry door is the oldest surviving door in Nottingham – dating to around 1380; more recent additions include the bronze doors installed in 1904.

St Mary's Church

0. NATIONAL JUSTICE MUSEUM

Housed in a former courtroom, prison and police station, this Victorian grade II* listed building was a one-stop shop where criminals could be processed from arrest through to execution.

While the first reference to a courtroom here is from 1375, it was officially a jail from at least 1449.

Until 1832 most public executions took place at Gallows Hill, with the last one held in 1864 when Richard Thomas Parker was hanged for shooting his parents, killing his mother.

10. PITCHER & PIANO

Originally an unassuming Unitarian chapel, built in 1805, this grand Gothic-style construction was erected in 1876.

Although feature wallpaper adorns the recesses, the conversion to a pub included reclaimed pews, original fireplaces and lacework that pays homage to its location at the heart of the lace market area.

Despite the confession box at this converted pub, what happens on the pub crawl stays on the pub crawl.

P. CITY OF CAVES EXHIBITION

This popular tourist attraction shares the story of the caves carved out of the sandstone ridge that Nottingham sits on.

As the stone could easily be cut using hand tools, people dug cellars into it. More than eight hundred caves have been discovered underneath the city, with the only known underground tannery in Britain originally dug out in 1250.

During World War II, many of the caves were joined to create large, public air-raid shelters; the excavated sand was used as ballast to protect the city.

LONDON
(Marylebone Loop)

Starting at the busy tourist hotspot of Oxford Street, this route winds north into the wealthy area of Marylebone among old buildings, occasional cobbled streets and rows of terraced houses.

Along the way you can take in Marylebone High Street, which has often been referred to as London's hidden gem, with its bustling atmosphere and celebrity residents.

Usually the local pubs in this area are among the quieter in London; some of them are closed on Sundays, although you can still find plenty of places to stop, take in the area and have a good meal.

I love how this route takes you away from the tourist spots into a rarely promoted part of London that includes some beautiful high-end establishments without being too pricey.

Start from Oxford Circus station (W1B 3AG).

1. **The Cock Tavern** *1.30 p.m.*
27 Great Portland Street, W1W 8QE

2. **The George** *2.00 p.m.*
55 Great Portland Street, W1W 7LQ

3. **The Wigmore** *3.00 p.m.*
15 Langham Place, W1B 3DE

4. **The Jackalope (closed Sunday)** *3.30 p.m.*
43 Weymouth Mews, W1G 7EQ

5. **The Cavendish** *4.15 p.m.*
35 New Cavendish Street, W1G 9TR

6. **Angel in the Fields** *5.00 p.m.*
37 Thayer Street, W1U 2QY

7. **Golden Eagle (closed Sunday)** *5.45 p.m.*
59 Marylebone Lane, W1U 2NY

8. **The Coach Makers Arms** *6.30 p.m.*
88 Marylebone Lane, W1U 2PZ

9. **The Cock & Lion** *7.15 p.m.*
62 Wigmore Street, W1U 2SA

10. **The Spread Eagle** *8.00 p.m.*
8 Woodstock Street, W1C 2AD

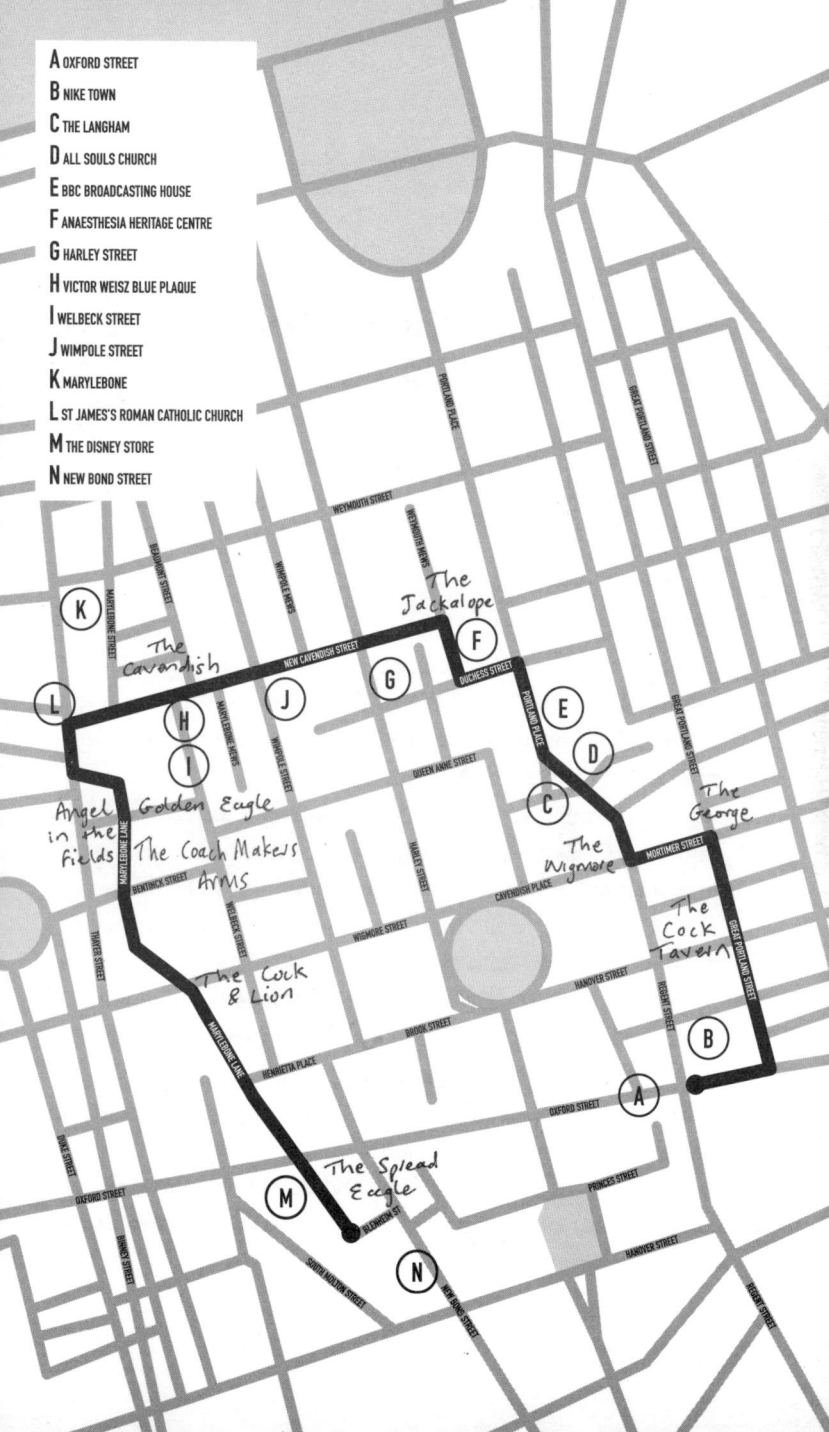

A OXFORD STREET
B NIKE TOWN
C THE LANGHAM
D ALL SOULS CHURCH
E BBC BROADCASTING HOUSE
F ANAESTHESIA HERITAGE CENTRE
G HARLEY STREET
H VICTOR WEISZ BLUE PLAQUE
I WELBECK STREET
J WIMPOLE STREET
K MARYLEBONE
L ST JAMES'S ROMAN CATHOLIC CHURCH
M THE DISNEY STORE
N NEW BOND STREET

DIRECTIONS

Leave the station **(A, B)** through the Argyll Road exit and head right a few paces before crossing the road and heading down where **The Cock Tavern (1)** is two blocks down on the corner. Continue past the pub, where **The George (2)** is further down the road on the left.

Exit the pub to the right, down Mortimer Street; **The Wigmore (3, C)** is on the opposite corner at the main road. Leave the hotel and turn left towards the church **(D, E, F)**, following the bend in the road. Take the left at Duchess Street before turning first right onto the cobbled mews. **The Jackalope (4)** is just down the road, almost opposite the end of the mews.

Retrace to New Cavendish Street and turn right **(G, H)** until reaching **The Cavendish (5)** on the corner. Continue along the road **(I, J)** then turn left at Marylebone High Street **(K, L)**, where **Angel in the Fields (6)** is left, along the road.

Follow the passageway along the side of the pub, and the road curves right. After the block paved road, **Golden Eagle (7)** is on the opposite side of the road at the end.

Continue along the block-paved road, past the Ivy café, to **The Coach Makers Arms (8)** on the left.

Follow the road as it curves left where **The Cock & Lion (9)** is on the left at the main road.

Leave the pub and head over the road, following it until it splits. Take the left path and upon reaching the high street **(M, N)**, cross over to the pedestrian area where the final pub **The Spread Eagle (10)** is on the left.

A. OXFORD STREET

This is Europe's busiest shopping street – with more than 500,000 visitors a day – and it was originally part of the Roman road between what are now Hampshire and Essex.

It was known as the Tyburn Road, after the river, through-out the Middle Ages. A notable point along the road, Tyburn Tree, was used for public executions of criminals. Nowadays, it is the location of Marble Arch.

It was not until around 1729 that the road became known as Oxford Street, as many of the surrounding fields were pur-chased by the Earl of Oxford.

Although a popular destination for entertainment due to its theatres, pubs and attractions such as bear-baiting, the area struggled to attract the upper-middle classes due to the nearby gallows and slums.

Towards the end of the eighteenth century the street shifted from residential to retail, with several large department stores being established over the next 150 years.

During World War II the street suffered heavy bombing, with many of the large stores severely damaged by direct hits or fires. The most significant was inflicted on John Lewis – which was established on the street in 1864 – and caused it to move to its current location.

Every year, since 1959, the street is decorated by Christmas lights which are often switched on by a celebrity towards the end of November. They were absent in 1976–77 due to an economic downturn. Festivities were postponed in 1963 after JFK's assassination and in 1989 to accommodate Kylie Minogue's touring commitments when she was selected for the switch-on. Some notable people to have taken the mantle are Madonna, Leona Lewis, Jim Carrey, Robbie Williams and S Club 7.

B. NIKE TOWN

One of the most globally recognised brands, Nike was founded as the 'Blue Ribbon Sports' company by Bill Bowerman and Phil Knight. Originally, it was the exclusive US distributor of Japanese brand Onitsuka Tiger, and they generated most of their sales from Knight's car boot at athletics events.

Their early shoe designs became famous due to a manufacturing process that included the use of Bowerman's waffle iron to create the distinctive 'waffle trainer' that replaced conventional spikes.

One of sports most iconic images, the 'Swoosh' logo was first used in 1971 after freelancer Carolyn Davidson created it for about $35. Three years after the company went public, CEO Phil Knight presented Davidson with a gift of 500 shares, which were worth $85 at the time but are now valued at several million dollars.

1. THE COCK TAVERN

Despite its poultry emblem, like many pubs of the time, it may have been named after the once popular Cock Ale.

The pub was first licensed in 1737, before the current building was constructed in 1898, and it is one of the few London pubs that retain 'snob screens' as well as original fixtures such as the back bar and fireplace surround. A snob screen is a set of decorated panes of glass that hide adjoining rooms in pubs from one another while still allowing a central bar to serve both rooms. This reportedly allowed the middle and upper classes to drink in establishments that also served the working class, without having to see them.

I was joined on the London route by YouTube's Craft Beer Channel *hosts Jonny and Brad.*

2. THE GEORGE

This grade II listed pub was the location for many historical movements in the late eighteenth century, and retains some of the original painted tiles featuring riders and dogs.

It was established in 1677 and rebuilt in 1878 at a total cost of £4,467. Its Gluepot Bar is called after the nickname bestowed by Sir Thomas Beecham due to the propensity of his musicians to 'keep getting stuck there.' Beecham was a conductor at the London Philharmonic and Royal Philharmonic orchestras, so he had a lot of musicians he may have lost to the George.

The rooms upstairs also have distinctive décor, with either bright red or bright green walls, depending on where you sit. It really is like few pubs you will see.

It's claimed to pour one of the capital's best pints of Guinness, and when we filmed that was what most customers were drinking.

Spotted even more frequently than me, the man better known as SchoonerScorer joined me for a pint.

3. THE WIGMORE

This upscale, distinctive green bar at the Langham Hotel was formerly a banking hall, but has now been refurbished and upscaled into this decadent gastropub.

When you pop in, keep an eye out for celebrities and broadcasters from the nearby BBC studios as this a popular hang-out.

I was lucky to film the pub with memorable *The Apprentice* candidate Nick Showering who, despite flopping on the show, went on to run his family's successful cider business.

I got to grab a drink with former BBC Apprentice *contestant Nick Showering, who now runs his family's cider business.*

C. THE LANGHAM

Built between 1863 and 1865 at a cost of £300,000 (equivalent to £32 million in 2025), this five-star hotel was the largest and most modern in London at the time.

It was opened by the then Prince Edward of Wales, who later became Edward VII, and it soon became a commercial success.

Several notable guests have frequented its 380 rooms and grand ballroom over the years, including members of the royal family, Winston Churchill, Noël Coward, Don Bradman and Oscar Wilde.

During the Great Depression its ownership passed to the BBC as additional accommodation for the adjacent Broadcasting House, but after planning permission to demolish the building was refused it was sold to Hilton owners Ladbroke Group for £26 million in 1991.

D. ALL SOULS CHURCH

This church was designed by one of the foremost British architects of the Georgian and Regency eras, John Nash, who was a favourite of King George IV. Other notable buildings by Nash include the Royal Pavilion in Brighton (see page 31) and Buckingham Palace.

The church was consecrated in 1824 and its location, next to BBC Broadcasting House, means it is often the location of religious events or occasions for television.

E. BBC BROADCASTING HOUSE

This headquarters for the British Broadcasting Corporation was first opened in 1932 and is the main location for all national BBC radio broadcasts – except for sports, which are broadcast from Media City in Salford Quays.

The grade II* listed building is constructed out of Portland stone in an Art Deco style. It is built in two parts, with a central core containing studios and the outer portion housing office and administrative departments.

From 2003, more of the BBC's operations were relocated here following extensive renovation work – this included the BBC World Service from Bush House and BBC News from Television Centre.

It was revealed in 1985 that the security service MI5 held a private office in the building from 1937, which was used to vet employees for national security.

BBC Broadcasting House

F. ANAESTHESIA HERITAGE CENTRE

A member of the London Museums of Health & Medicine group, the centre's museum contains more than 4,500 objects and artefacts dating back to 1774.

It traces the history of anaesthesia, resuscitation and pain relief, with examples of equipment and procedures.

4. THE JACKALOPE

The mythical North American animal this pub takes its name from is said to have the body of a jackrabbit and the antlers of an antelope. It's thought the legends stemmed from a group of rabbits around Wyoming that had been infected with Shope papilloma virus, which causes tumours that look like horns to grow in various places on a rabbit's body.

While the legends have existed for centuries, they became more prominent in the Americas when taxidermists the Herrick brothers began grafting deer antlers onto carcasses and selling them into retail outlets in the 1930s.

The pub itself has been here since 1777, and its old name, Dover Castle, is etched into the windows. It was originally divided with a beam, with mirrors strategically placed to allow coachmen to see when their passengers were ready to depart.

G. HARLEY STREET

Named after the 2nd Earl of Oxford, the street has become notorious in recent years due to its large number of cosmetic surgery offices and their celebrity clientele.

Originally, there were around twenty doctors operating on the street, but that number rose to two hundred between 1860 and 1914. Today more than three thousand people are employed on or around the street.

There have been hundreds of notable residents over the years, including knights, lords, ladies and politicians. The street is also a popular destination for those wanting to explore feminist history, as both Florence Nightingale and Nancy Astor (the first woman to sit in Parliament) both lived on the street.

5. THE CAVENDISH

This pub is located on New Cavendish Street, which was once home to Alfred Waterhouse. Waterhouse was a famous architect, best known as the designer of the Natural History Museum.

The street was built in 1775 and named after the Cavendish

family, who were related to landowners the Dukes of Portland.

I've fond memories of this place as I brought my family here for a special Sunday roast where my children got involved in filming the pub for our social media channels.

The pub can be a great place for a special occasion. Here my two boys, Vincent (left) and Ellis, take their mom out for Mother's Day.

H. VICTOR WEISZ BLUE PLAQUE

A German–British political cartoonist, Victor Weisz was widely known under his pen name, Vicky, and worked from the early 1920s to his death in 1966.

During their rise to power, Weisz was vocally against the Nazi Party and their regime. When they took office, he was among the first to leave Germany. His work often satirised the party and its leader, so Weisz subsequently became one of the leading left-wing cartoonists in the UK. His work appeared in the *News Chronicle*, *Daily Mirror* and *Evening Standard*.

Weisz's father took his own life in 1928 and, thirty-eight years later, after a lifetime of battles with depression and insomnia, Weisz also took his own life aged just fifty-two.

I. WELBECK STREET

Like Harley Street, this road is linked to the medical profession.

Its notable past residents have included eighteenth-century highwayman James MacLaine, who once ran a grocer's here, physician Thomas Young, who established his clinic here in 1799, and the seemingly fearless Andrew Berry, one of the first men to successfully deploy a parachute at an altitude of less than 3,000 feet – usually a skydiver will pull their chute between 3,000 and 5,000 feet.

It was a tough task to chaperone aspiring young politician Jay Chan as he set himself the task of downing a pint in every constituency in the country to support the pub industry.

J. WIMPOLE STREET

Home to the Royal Society of Medicine and the headquarters of the British Dental Association, the street name comes from the Cambridgeshire estate owned by the Harley family. The family developed the street into what it is today, introducing infrastructure and living on it themselves.

Paul McCartney lived here with Jane Asher in the 1960s

and it was here that he wrote 'I Want to Hold Your Hand' with John Lennon, and 'Yesterday' alone.

Other notable residents include the creator of Sherlock Holmes, Arthur Conan Doyle, who worked at 2 Upper Wimpole Street during 1891 and has been commemorated with a green plaque. Elizabeth Barrett also lived here before eloping with Robert Browning. Both husband and wife became famous in the literary world, as well as campaigning for human rights.

K. MARYLEBONE

This former parish was created to serve the manors of Lisson Grove and Tyburn, and there has been an ancient parish here since at least the twelfth century.

The parish system was established and widespread between the eighth and twelfth centuries, and was often based on Roman boundaries or Iron Age settlements. It was a system to ensure everybody went to church, by assigning certain areas to certain religious buildings. This sometimes led to wonky boundaries, as some churches could handle larger congregations than others, so people did not necessarily go to the one closest to them.

It takes its name from an ancient hamlet near the Tyburn River, where St Mary's Church was built in the 1400s. Over the years the name adapted to include 'burne' – an old word for a small stream – and 'le' from Mary-le-Bow.

The locals eventually settled on St Mary-le-bourne after other iterations including Mariburn, Marybone, Marrowbone and Marie la Bonne. Over time this developed into the current iteration.

In 2002, BBC Radio 4 listeners voted the high street the best in London.

L. ST JAMES'S ROMAN CATHOLIC CHURCH

This large Gothic church has enjoyed a close historic connection to the Spanish Embassy ever since it was completed in 1890. The ambassador, his family and his staff traditionally worshipped here. Because of this, other Spanish immigrants and tourists came here too.

Its entrance, via George Street, is a copy of Lichfield Cathedral, while the interior design has taken inspiration from Salisbury Cathedral and Westminster Abbey.

The original palace and chapel were lent to the Spanish ambassador until the reign of Charles I when diplomatic relationships with the country ended. Later, the restoration of Charles II re-established the embassy in London.

Although the Spanish connection ceased in 1827, much of the present building pays homage to its Spanish heritage – including Alfonso XIII's personal standard, which hangs over the sacristy door.

6. ANGEL IN THE FIELDS

A striking pub with a wooden frontage; the stained-glass windows are widely acknowledged as some of London's most beautiful.

7. GOLDEN EAGLE

This old-style Marylebone pub was first licensed in 1842 before being rebuilt at the end of the nineteenth century.

A CAMRA award winner, it is well known for its piano sing-a-long evenings which have been running three nights a week since 1988, stopping only for Covid-19.

8. THE COACH MAKERS ARMS

A regular contender for *Time Out* 'Best Gastropub', it was re-opened in 2017 under the Cubitt House management group and contains a basement speakeasy.

Beer and pizza is a great combo and here I am enjoying Slice-o-Mania with fat_boi_ldn before heading off on the next crawl.

9. THE COCK & LION

The oldest pub in Marylebone, dating back to 1786, it has all the traditional features of the time, with a distinctive horse-shoe-shaped bar.

It was formerly known as the Lyon and Cock and claimed it was the only pub in the country with that name.

M. THE DISNEY STORE

The Walt Disney Company, founded in 1923 as the Disney Brothers Cartoon Studio, first rose to fame in 1928 with their animation *Steamboat Willie*, which featured the iconic Mickey Mouse. They pioneered a new technology that synchronised sound with movement. Since then they've created many beloved characters, including Donald Duck, Goofy and Minnie Mouse.

The company's early success in the 1940s led to it diversifying into theme parks, television and live-action films.

After creator Walt Disney's death in 1966, the company's fortunes began to decline until the former president of rival Paramount Pictures, Michael Eisner, took over in 1984. Eisner spearheaded a renaissance of animation that ultimately led to their corporate efforts to expand into a major entertainment conglomerate – acquiring the likes of Pixar, Marvel, Lucasfilm and 21st Century Fox.

It operates several steaming, broadcasting, publishing, international and consumer product divisions.

As one of the best-known companies in the world, it has won 135 Academy Awards, produced some of the greatest movies of all time, and revolutionised the theme park industry.

After the company opened a chain of branded retail stores in 1987, London became the site of its first overseas store in 1990. In March 2021 the company announced the closure of more than 150 stores and a strategic shift towards e-commerce operations. The London store survived this cull, and can still be enjoyed today.

N. NEW BOND STREET

Built on the fields owned by Sir Thomas Bond from the 1720s, it became a popular haunt of wealthy Mayfair residents.

In recent years it has become one of the most expensive real estate locations in the world. It is also the location of several prestigious retail brands, including the jeweller Tiffany & Co.

and world-renowned auction houses Sotheby's and Bonhams.

The street features the sculpture *Allies*, which depicts Winston Churchill and Franklin D. Roosevelt sitting in conversation on a park bench. It was erected by the Bond Street Association to commemorate fifty years since the end of World War II, and was unveiled by Princess Margaret in 1995.

10. THE SPREAD EAGLE

Although fairly new by London standards, having been rebuilt in 1955, there has been a pub on this site since the seventeenth century.

It was mentioned in Maurice Gorham's 1949 book *Back to the Local*, which made the barmaids famous with the line 'two dizzy blondes both sprang forward as soon as you opened the door'. I can't help but wonder if they were still springing after all that attention and extra work.

NEWCASTLE to GATESHEAD

Starting at the station, close to the city centre, the route ambles under the imposing shadow of one of the UK's most famous bridges before crossing the Tyne and heading up the steep path to the edge of Gateshead.

Newcastle has hundreds of pubs, and this collection mixes the impressive station pub with the medieval buildings by the riverbank. The route includes Newcastle's oldest pub, which is also one of the oldest in the country.

It comes as no surprise that the locals are all friendly and will spend time with you, especially if you are from out of town.

Be sure to avoid match days, though, as this one-club city is usually heaving.

Start at Newcastle upon Tyne station (NE1 5DL).

1. **The Centurion** *1.00 p.m.*
Central Station, NE1 5DG

2. **The Victoria Comet** *1.30 p.m.*
38 Neville Street, NE1 5DF

3. **The Forth** *2.15 p.m.*
Pink Lane, NE1 5DW

4. **The Beehive** *3.00 p.m.*
2 High Bridge, NE1 1EN

5. **Old George Inn** *3.30 p.m.*
Old George Yard, NE1 1EZ

6. **Bacchus** *4.15 p.m.*
42–48 High Bridge, NE1 6BX

7. **Crown Posada** *5.00 p.m.*
31 Side Street, NE1 3JE

8. **Redhouse** *5.45 p.m.*
32 Sandhill, NE1 3JF

9. **The Dubliner** *6.30 p.m.*
12 Close, NE1 3RE

10. **Lock and Quay (closed Mondays)** *7.15 p.m.*
1 Pipewellgate, NE8 2BJ

11. **The Central** *8.00 p.m.*
Half Moon Lane, NE8 2AN

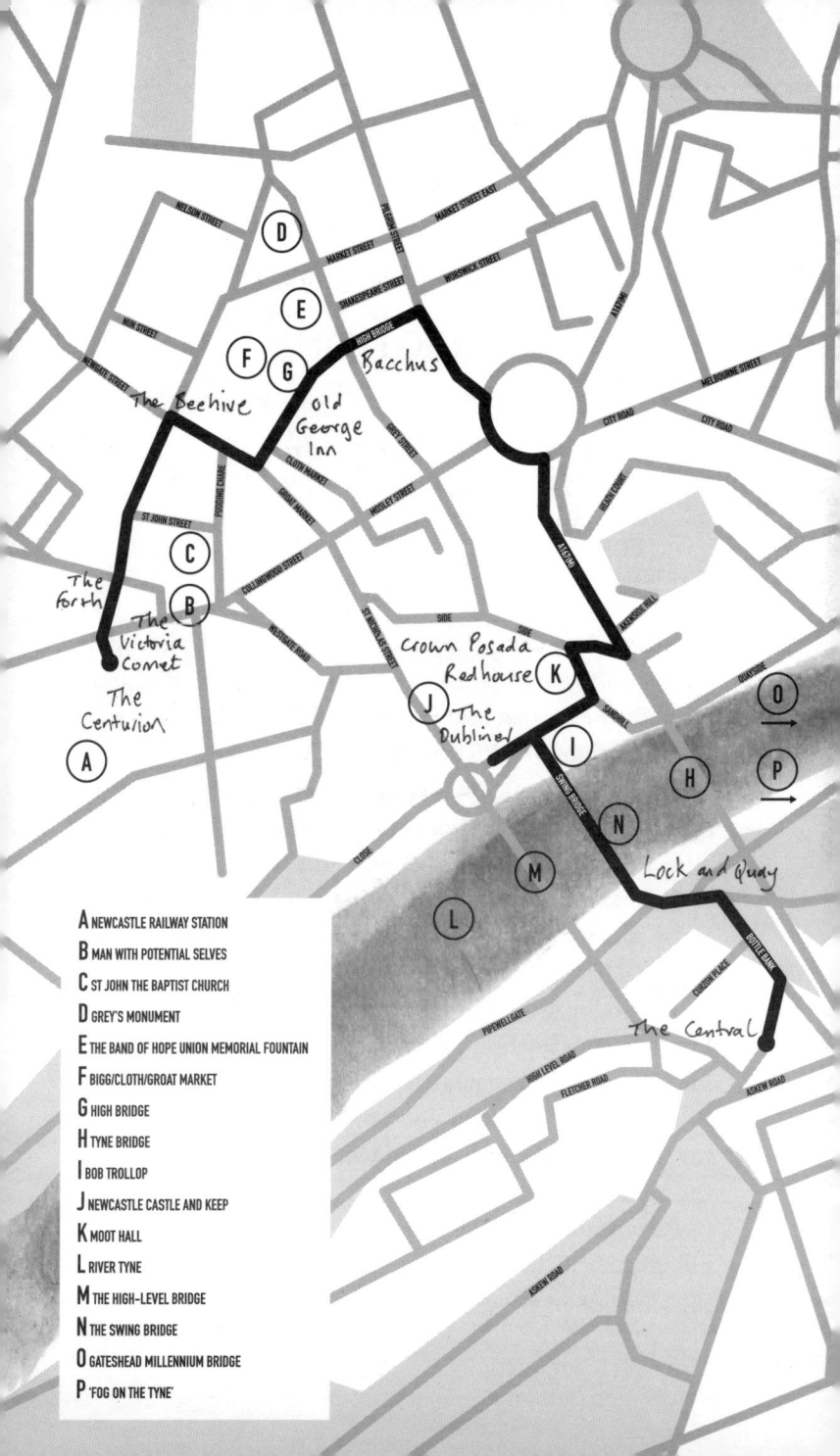

A NEWCASTLE RAILWAY STATION

B MAN WITH POTENTIAL SELVES

C ST JOHN THE BAPTIST CHURCH

D GREY'S MONUMENT

E THE BAND OF HOPE UNION MEMORIAL FOUNTAIN

F BIGG/CLOTH/GROAT MARKET

G HIGH BRIDGE

H TYNE BRIDGE

I BOB TROLLOP

J NEWCASTLE CASTLE AND KEEP

K MOOT HALL

L RIVER TYNE

M THE HIGH-LEVEL BRIDGE

N THE SWING BRIDGE

O GATESHEAD MILLENNIUM BRIDGE

P 'FOG ON THE TYNE'

DIRECTIONS

On arrival, **The Centurion (1)** can be found inside the station on the north side **(A)**. Exit the pub to the main road, turn left at the pedestrian area **(B)** and walk parallel to the station before reaching **The Victoria Comet (2)**.

The first alleyway, after leaving the pub and heading right, is Pink Lane where **The Forth (3)** is on the corner halfway up. Turn right out of the pub, along Forth Lane, and turn right at the main road, before taking the second left up Grainger Street past St John the Baptist Church **(C)**, with Grey's Monument **(D)** in the distance.

Turn right at the first junction onto the market square **(E, F)**, where **The Beehive (4)** is on the corner and **Old George Inn (5)** down an alley just a few yards past it.

Head out of the other end of the alley, and turn right on the main road up High Bridge **(G)**, where **Bacchus (6)** is on the right.

Past the pub, turn right on the main road and go down the hill, sticking to the right-hand side of the pavement. Continue over the roundabout before taking the steps on the right, immediately before crossing Tyne Bridge **(H)**.

Turn left at the road, and cross the roundabout to the left. **Crown Posada (7)** is over the road, with **Redhouse (8, I)** a few doors down.

Exit the pub and continue along the quayside, passing the alleyway on the right to the castle, keep **(J)** and Moot Hall **(K)** before reaching **The Dubliner (9)**.

Retrace your steps before crossing the river **(L, M)** using the swing bridge **(N)**, with the white Gateshead Millennium Bridge **(O, P)** in the distance, to find **Lock and Quay (10)** on the other side. Follow the road up the hill and take the first right before reaching **The Central (11)** on the corner before the main road.

1. THE CENTURION

This extravagant pub was built in 1893 as a waiting room for the railway's first-class passengers, before it was closed in the 1960s and converted into holding cells for the British Transport Police. You would never know looking at it now, as the high ceilings and open floor plan are the opposite of the small, cramped jail that used to be here.

After years of neglect, it was restored, and its exquisite tile work is worth an estimated £3.8 million.

This is probably the most surprised and impressed I have been walking into a pub, because the unremarkable exterior just doesn't prepare you for the beautifully designed bar inside.

The Centurion Bar

A. NEWCASTLE RAILWAY STATION

Opened in 1850 as part of the then Newcastle & Carlisle Railway and the York, Newcastle & Berwick Railway, it was initially called the Central railway station. It was designed by the neoclassical architect John Dobson, who was responsible for more than fifty churches and a hundred private houses as well as this station.

The scheme to construct the station was proposed as early as 1836 before the 'Railway King', politician and rail financier George Hudson, obtained authorisation to connect the local networks through an act of parliament.

The train shed was, along with Liverpool Lime Street, the first to be designed using wrought-iron ribs supporting an arched roof. The exterior of the station was in the Romano-Italian style.

The day it was opened by Queen Victoria was declared a public holiday in the city.

B. MAN WITH POTENTIAL SELVES

This piece of public art consists of three statues along the pedestrian area of Lower Grainger Street.

Sculptor Sean Henry, who typically focuses on the human form, has dubbed the three creations Standing Man, Walking Man and Floating Man – with the installations meant to represent the alter egos of the same everyman character. Henry is known for his work depicting the everyday people of Britain, and became a favourite of one of my assistants when he had an extended showcase in her home-town cathedral in Ely.

2. THE VICTORIA COMET

Originally this building hosted two pubs – the Victoria and the Comet – from the 1800s, but the two merged to form a hotel.

After being closed for decades, it was restored and is now run as the Nicholson's pub chain's northernmost location.

It is notable for its inclusion in the 1971 cult gangster movie *Get Carter* as the first stop on returning to the city for the Newcastle-born hitman played by Michal Caine.

Although initially met with a lukewarm reception, the film gained cult status after the endorsements of legendary directors Guy Ritchie and Quentin Tarantino – leading to *Total Film* magazine ranking it as the greatest British film of all time.

3. THE FORTH

This city centre pub is split across several levels, with nooks and crannies throughout and a secluded roof terrace.

In the 1920s it was owned by former world heavyweight boxing champion Tommy Burns, who is best remembered as the man Jack Johnson defeated to become the first Black heavyweight champ. Born Noah Brusso in Ontario, Canada, Burns is widely acknowledged as a travelling fighter, making thirteen title defences against eleven different boxers.

As of 2025 he remains the only Canadian-born heavyweight champion in history. His small 5'7" stature was unusual for a heavyweight and often meant he was seen as the underdog.

He is the shortest heavyweight champion in history and the second lightest. Despite his stature, his 74-inch reach is 3 inches longer than hall-of-fame champion 'Iron' Mike Tyson.

His determination to take on all challengers is summed up by his insistence to his biographer that:

I will defend my title against all comers, none barred.
By this I mean white, black, Mexican, Indian, or any
other nationality. I propose to be the champion of the
world, not the white, or the Canadian, or the American.
If I am not the best man in the heavyweight division,
I don't want the title.

C. ST JOHN THE BAPTIST CHURCH

Built around 1287, this grade I listed building is dedicated to St John the Baptist, who was a Jewish preacher active around the River Jordan in the early first century.

Much of the current stone is a copy of the original, which was removed during 1861 restorations.

Now nestled in the heart of the city, parts of the graveyard were built over, leaving just ten gravestones visible. Try not to think about what that means is under your feet as you're walking past. Of the gravestones that survived, one belongs to Irish actor and poet John Cunningham, who spent much of his life in Newcastle.

D. GREY'S MONUMENT

Built in 1838 to recognise the 2nd Earl Grey, who was prime minister between 1830 and 1834, this monument celebrates the passing of one of his most important legislative achievements – the Great Reform Act of 1832. This act redistributed parliamentary seats, reduced the influence of corrupt areas and made the electoral system fairer by increasing the number of those eligible to vote. It allowed many more working-class men to vote, although it explicitly barred women from voting at the time.

E. THE BAND OF HOPE UNION MEMORIAL FOUNTAIN

Relocated in the early twentieth century, this ornate drinking fountain was erected in 1894 in memory of J. H. Rutherford, who was an evangelical preacher and founder of the School of Science and Art.

F. BIGG/CLOTH/GROAT MARKET

Dating back to the Middle Ages, this once thriving market square formed an important sector of the Great North Road.

Bigg is a distinctive variety of barley; groats are oats without husks. Both lend their name to the market, alongside simple cloth. The old town hall building from 1863 was located here and remained the meeting place for the city council until 1968.

In modern times the build-up of bars and nightclubs at the edges of the open space has given the area a reputation for disorderly, drunken behaviour.

4. THE BEEHIVE

This grade II listed corner pub was built in 1902 and is notable for its distinctive glazed green faience tiling on the exterior.

Above the single-room pub are three storeys of office space, topped by a Persian-style ogee tower. Ogee is an architectural term, referring to a sort of serpentine or s-shape.

It's notable for being one of the cheapest places in Newcastle, if not the UK, to grab a pint: as cheap as £2 at the time of going to print.

One of the cheapest places in the country to buy a pint, although on my visit I went for the local gin.

5. OLD GEORGE INN

The oldest pub in Newcastle, it was built in 1582 and is rumoured to have been frequented by King Charles I while he was exiled in a nearby open prison.

The chair he supposedly sat in is still in the pub, and there have been reports of ghostly figures in his corner. Patrons are encouraged to keep an eye on the seat as they drink.

Hidden down a cobbled alleyway, the old stables are now outdoor seating and the higgledy-piggledy layout of the building, with uneven floors and bowing walls, adds to the pub's haunted atmosphere.

G. HIGH BRIDGE

There was only one lane linking the market streets to Pilgrim Street in the late eighteenth century, in part because of the steep angle of the Lort Burn (a subterranean stream) that lay between them and the bridge. As both sides of the lane were built up, the High Bridge crossed the Burn, leaving a noticeable dip in the road outside numbers 31–37.

6. BACCHUS

There have been three different city pubs called the Bacchus – after the Roman god of wine and pleasure.

The original pub survived from 1822 to 1971, before it was demolished, along with many other buildings, to make way for a new shopping centre.

The current version is a sports bar in the style of a grand ocean liner, with naval décor among the large-screen TVs.

H. TYNE BRIDGE

Only the tenth-tallest structure in Newcastle, it has become the city's defining symbol since it was opened by King George V in 1928.

Several bridges have spanned the Tyne at this location, with the earliest wooden structure believed to have been built around AD 122.

It was not until the thirteenth century that stone bridges were constructed, with several suffering severe storm damage. As modern engineering techniques developed, work on the current bridge commenced in 1925.

It was designed by Mott, Hay and Anderson, who were also involved in the design of Sydney Harbour Bridge and the Channel Tunnel.

In preparation for the city's involvement in the London 2012 Olympics – hosting football matches and the torch relay – the largest Olympic rings in the UK were erected and installed on the bridge.

Tyne Bridge

7. CROWN POSADA

This narrow three-storey pub was rebuilt in 1880 for the local brewer John Sanderson and was one of the most highly recommended pubs by my social media followers when I said I was coming to the city.

Behind the stirring Pre-Raphaelite-style stained-glass windows (believed to be by renowned Birmingham artist Edward Burne-Jones), there are three distinct drinking areas, including a snug to the front.

It was renamed from the Crown by a Spanish naval captain in honour of his mistress; *posada* is the Spanish word for resting place.

The pub has seen several refurbishments, although all have attempted to stay true to the original look of the bar.

One unique thing is that the music in the pub comes from a 1941 turntable at the end of the bar, with patrons encouraged to bring their own vinyl LPs to play.

8. REDHOUSE

This medieval building, held together by pattress plates, is one of the oldest buildings in the city and is distinctive for its uneven red frontage. The wedge-shaped grade II* listed structure rises five floors and has stone lintels over traditional sash windows.

My camera assistant Maddie and I stopped here to eat on our days filming, and not only does it serve fantastic pies, but its seemingly endless corridors and nooks and crannies make the place feel exactly as old and medieval as it is.

I. BOB TROLLOP

This old timbered bar is part of the Redhouse pub building, with the eponymous Trollop renowned as one of Newcastle's more prominent architects, having built Newcastle's Exchange and Guildhall between 1655 and 1658.

He was born into a family of stonemasons, and worked predominantly across Northumberland and County Durham.

J. NEWCASTLE CASTLE AND KEEP

Built on the site of the castle that gave the city its name, the most prominent structures that remain are the castle's main fortified tower and its gatehouse. Initially it was a wooden motte-and-bailey castle, on the site of the ancient Roman fort, before Henry II built a stone keep around 1177. All very 'new', these castles.

Sometime around 1250 the 'Black Gate' was constructed to add a barbican (a fortified outpost) to the north of the castle. While the original construction would probably have had a flat roof, it was substantially altered when James I leased it to Alexander Stephenson who subsequently sublet it to merchant Patrick Black, who gave it the current name. The flat roof would have been easier to build, but would have been more prone to damage and leaks.

During the English Civil War, in 1643, the Royalist mayor of Newcastle, Sir John Marley, repaired the keep and refortified the castle in case his city was ever attacked.

His fear proved right; as the Scottish army crossed the border in support of the Parliamentarians, they besieged Newcastle for several months until the garrison surrendered after the town walls had been extensively damaged.

The buildings fell into disrepair over the next two hundred years and were repurposed as a jail; many houses were later constructed in the castle boundaries.

The Castle Keep

K. MOOT HALL

This Greek revival building is a former courthouse that was completed in 1812 on the site of a Roman fort – during excavations, two coins from the time of Emperor Antoninus Pius and two Roman altars were discovered.

Several notable trials have taken place here, such as that of Scottish serial killer Robert Black, who murdered four young girls between 1981 and 1986; and eleven-year-old Mary Bell, for the murder of two young boys in 1968. The latter is notable for being Britain's youngest female killer. Controversially, in 1980 she was released, at the age of twenty-three, and has lived in anonymity ever since. She would be in her late sixties as of 2025.

9. THE DUBLINER

Newcastle Quayside's first Irish bar, this lively music venue was converted from Julie's nightclub, which was one of the city's most iconic bars in the 1970s and regularly hosed the entire Newcastle United football team.

While we were visiting, they played the Dubliners, which most people found amusing, but was an annoyance to one particularly grouchy guest.

L. RIVER TYNE

Although only 73 miles in length, the river's large catchment area covers over 2,700 miles of waterways.

Its main source is in Alston Moor in Cumbria, with the mouth in Tynemouth, and it is estimated to be around 30 million years old.

M. THE HIGH-LEVEL BRIDGE

Constructed from over 5,000 tons of iron, it was opened in 1849 by Queen Victoria.

Son of the 'Father of the Railways', George Stephenson, Robert Stephenson designed the bridge to form a link towards Scotland for the developing railway network.

The impressive height of 120 feet above the water level accommodates the junction at Gateshead, and a two-tier layout was selected to avoid excessively wide foundations.

Despite the considerable increase in freight and traffic since its construction, it continues to function without full-scale renovations being necessary, albeit with a weight restriction.

N. THE SWING BRIDGE

At the time of its opening, in 1876, it was the largest swing bridge ever built and was constructed after the previous bridge had to be demolished to allow larger ships to reach the Armstrong Whitworth manufacturing works further upstream.

Now hardly used – it opens for pleasure boats or once a month for maintenance – at its peak in the 1920s it turned 6,000 times a year.

O. GATESHEAD MILLENNIUM BRIDGE

Sometimes nicknamed the Winking Eye or the Blinking Eye, it is the first tilting bridge ever constructed.

It was conceived when the local councils developed the nearby area to include new law courts and a contemporary arts centre, and there was a need to install a footbridge between the two cities.

More than 150 entries were filed in a competition to design the new bridge, with WilkinsonEyre architects and Gifford and Partners engineers claiming the prize.

Despite the joint project costing £22 million of Newcastle City Council money, Gateshead Council decided to name the bridge 'Gateshead Millennium Bridge', resulting in an ongoing feud between the two councils.

P. 'FOG ON THE TYNE'

The title track from the 1971 album from rock band Lindisfarne was heavily reworked in 1990 and released in collaboration with England footballer Paul Gascoigne after his rise in popularity at the World Cup in Italy.

The original album went to number one in the UK on its release. Nearly twenty years later, the Gascoigne version of the song peaked at number two.

10. LOCK AND QUAY

Recently opened, this new pub's terrace provides spectacular views over the river and of Newcastle's bridges.

It is housed in the old police station that spent some time as the acclaimed River Beat restaurant until the pub relaunch.

11. THE CENTRAL

This three-storey building was constructed in 1854 and is affectionately known as the Coffin due to its wedge shape.

It became a railway hotel in the 1890s and a subsequent refit in 1901 saw the installation of an impressive U-shaped counter bar in the now whisky room.

The seating at the point of the building is believed to be from the 1950s.

It is one of my absolute favourite pubs in the UK, because of the accommodating bar team, as well as its distinctive lay-out and unique atmosphere.

The best place to sit in the pub is at the end of the 'coffin'.

YORK
(River to Minster)

This cathedral city is famous for its Roman and Viking history and is filled with old buildings, monuments and pubs.

The narrow, cobbled market streets lined with overhanging timber-framed shops are unique in the country. The medieval aesthetic allows you to forget the speed and stress of the modern world.

The city is always filled with sightseers exploring the Jorvik Viking Centre, food markets and independent stores.

It rained heavily all day when we revisited to film the pubs, but with a pub on almost every corner it was the perfect place to hide by a warm fire (in the company of a ghost or two).

Featuring old, classic and quirky market town pubs, there is always something new to discover on this route.

Start at York station (YO26 4ZD).

1. **York Tap** *1.30 p.m.*
Station Road, YO24 1AB

2. **The Windmill** *2.00 p.m.*
14–16 Blossom Street, YO24 1AJ

3. **Kings Arms** *2.45 p.m.*
3 King's Staith, YO1 9SN

4. **Blue Boar** *3.15 p.m.*
5 Castlegate, YO1 9RN

5. **The Three Tuns** *4.00 p.m.*
12 Coppergate, YO1 9NR

6. **Ye Olde Shambles Tavern** *4.45 p.m.*
44 Shambles, YO1 7LX

7. **The Market Cat** *5.30 p.m.*
6 Jubbergate, YO1 8RT

8. **The Old White Swan** *6.15 p.m.*
80 Goodramgate, YO1 7LF

Snickleway Inn
47 Goodramgate, YO1 7LS

9. **The Habit** *7.00 p.m.*
40 Goodramgate, YO1 7LF

10. **The Royal Oak** *7.45 p.m.*
18 Goodramgate, YO1 7LG

11. **House of the Trembling Madness** *8.30 p.m.*
48 Stonegate, YO1 8AS

12. **Ye Olde Starre Inne** *9.15 p.m.*
40 Stonegate, YO1 8AS

13. **The Punch Bowl** *10.00 p.m.*
7 Stonegate, YO1 8AN

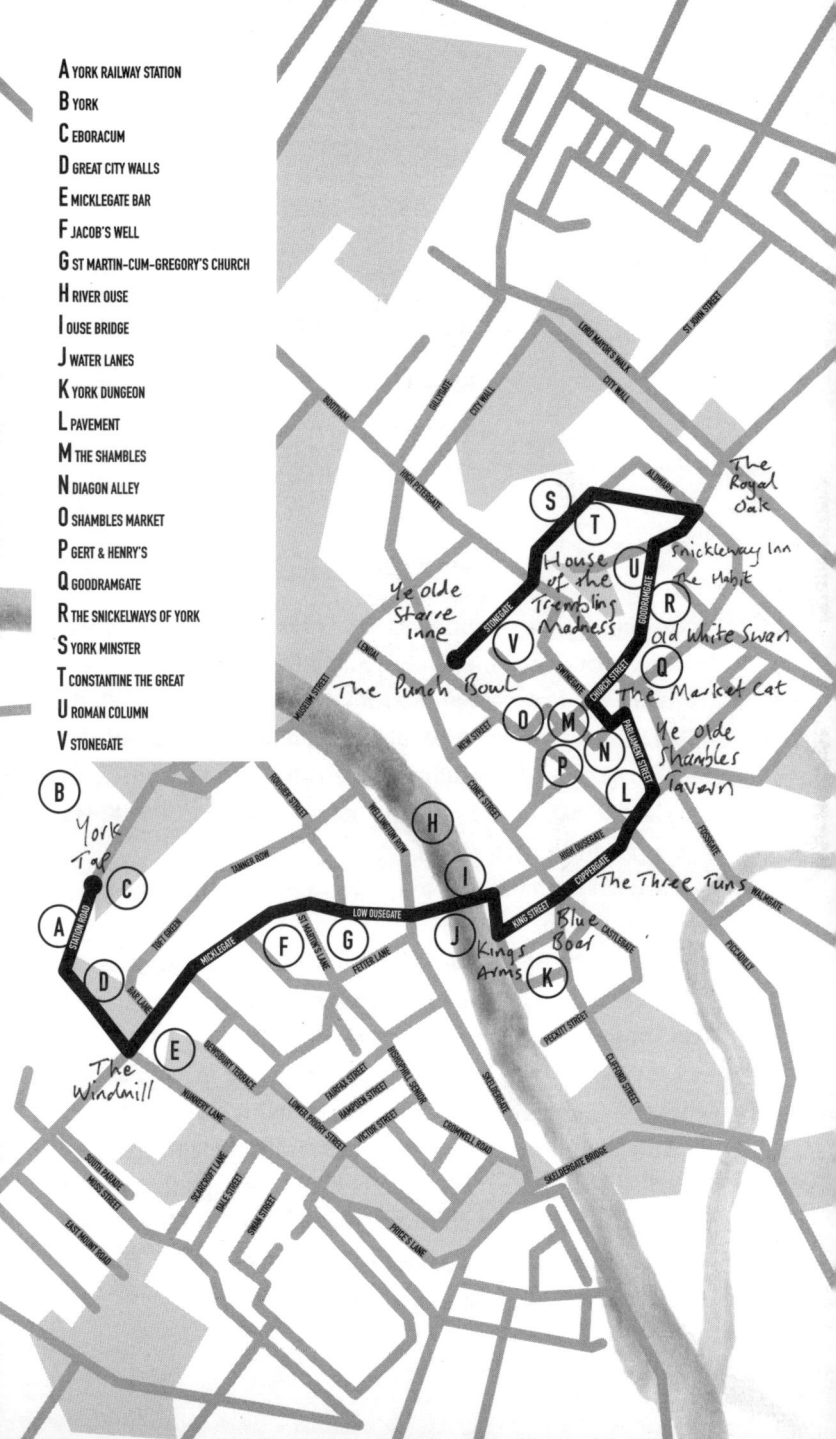

A YORK RAILWAY STATION
B YORK
C EBORACUM
D GREAT CITY WALLS
E MICKLEGATE BAR
F JACOB'S WELL
G ST MARTIN–CUM–GREGORY'S CHURCH
H RIVER OUSE
I OUSE BRIDGE
J WATER LANES
K YORK DUNGEON
L PAVEMENT
M THE SHAMBLES
N DIAGON ALLEY
O SHAMBLES MARKET
P GERT & HENRY'S
Q GOODRAMGATE
R THE SNICKELWAYS OF YORK
S YORK MINSTER
T CONSTANTINE THE GREAT
U ROMAN COLUMN
V STONEGATE

DIRECTIONS

Accessible via the station platform **(A)** is **York Tap (1)**. When leaving, turn right along Queen Street **(B, C)**.

As the road curves left, past the city walls **(D)**, **The Windmill (2)** is on the corner of the junction overlooking Micklegate Bar **(E)**. Head through the gatehouse with the church on the right **(F, G)**, before crossing the river **(H, I)** to **The Kings Arms (3)**, down a few steps.

Turn left from the pub and head away from the river along King Street **(J)** before taking the second right at the first junction **(K)** where **Blue Boar (4)** is a few yards along Castlegate. Leave the pub to return to the junction and turn right to find **The Three Tuns (5)** on the right of the road.

Leaving the pub turn right and cross the first junction, where the entrance to the Shambles **(M, N)** is on the left, with **Ye Olde Shambles Tavern (6)** a short walk along the path.

Exit through the rear of the pub and through the market **(O)**, heading slightly left, where **The Market Cat (7)** is on the opposite side. Follow Newgate to the rear of Gert & Henry's

(P), continuing through an alleyway and turning left as it reaches the road, before taking the first right **(Q)**, where **The Old White Swan (8)** is a few yards up on the left.

Continue past the pub, where **The Snickleway Inn (R)** and **The Habit (9)** are opposite each other, before following the road around right, where the mock-Tudor **The Royal Oak (10)** is on the opposite side of the road.

Turn right out of the pub, and follow the road around York Minster **(S)**, taking the pathway on the right in the grounds, past Constantine the Great **(T)** and the Roman Column **(U)**.

Follow the path, between buildings, opposite the minster and cross to Stonegate **(V)** where **House of the Trembling Madness (11)** is on the right, a couple of doors before **Ye Olde Starre Inne (12)** which is down any alley marked by a sign across the road. Continue along to **The Punch Bowl (13)**.

A. YORK RAILWAY STATION

One of only ten stations to be awarded five stars in Simon Jenkins's *Britain's 100 Best Railway Stations*, it is the busiest in North Yorkshire.

It was opened in 1877, replacing the old station that had become a hindrance to the high-speed, long-distance lines.

It took six years to complete construction and, at the time it opened, it was the largest railway station in the world, with thirteen platforms and a hotel. Nowadays, Grand Central station in New York holds that title, with a staggering forty-four platforms.

1. YORK TAP

Originally a fashionable tea room for the middle and upper classes (who would have been the only people able to afford rail travel at the time), this Edwardian building was converted into a pub in 2011. It was built within the station between 1872 and 1877.

It is notable for a large island bar, Art Deco stained-glass windows, terrazzo floors and an original stained-glass central ceiling dome.

It's a great way to start the route, but as we were only in York for a day, it also made for the perfect place to finish up with a few more beers while waiting for the train home.

A great place to start the route; we were unaware that it would be chucking it down all day.

B. YORK

A city that dates back to the Roman conquest, it was the capital of the Roman province of Britannia Inferior, and later the kingdoms of Deira and Northumbria.

Evidence suggests that there were temporary settlements in the region as far back as 8000 BC, when it was inhabited by the Mesolithic people of the Stone Age.

The location was targeted by invaders, as it was strategically significant for whoever held it. It provided a stronghold in the north, and in more modern times it has become a key railway location. In fact, the railway become one of the city's main industries. Another was confectionery, as both Rowntree's and Terry's had their headquarters here at the turn of the twentieth century; both the KitKat and Terry's Chocolate Orange were invented in York.

In 1942, the city was heavily bombed as part of the Baedeker Blitz – named after a series of German tourist guide books that mapped the city (among others) – and many of its iconic buildings were severely damaged.

Following efforts to repair the buildings, it became a tourist hub and was designated a conservation area in 1968.

C. EBORACUM

At the time the largest town in northern Britain, this Roman fort eventually developed into the present-day city of York.

Its first mention was around AD 100, and it is believed to have been founded in AD 70, roughly thirty years after the start of the Roman conquest of Britain.

A significant Roman stronghold, there is evidence it was visited by several emperors, notably being the place where both Septimius Severus and Constantius Chlorus died, in 211 and 306, respectively.

The Ouse and Foss rivers provided good transport links and it was known as a busy port that offered a diverse range of products.

D. GREAT CITY WALLS

With more miles of intact wall than any other city in England, York has been a defended medieval city for around two thousand years. Although the walls were probably more useful in 867 than they are in 2025.

Although often referred to as Roman walls, very little of the stonework is of Roman origin, as substantial changes have been made since their original construction around AD 71.

They were initially constructed as defences for the fort on the banks of the River Ouse, before the Danes came to occupy the city in 867.

The majority of the walls date from around the thirteenth and fourteenth centuries. They are punctuated by four gate-houses (known as 'bars', although not the kind we tour in this book) that were used to regulate traffic and collect taxes, tolls or fees.

2. THE WINDMILL

Reportedly haunted by the ghost of a young girl who was run over by a brewer's horse and cart, staff and patrons claim to have seen a rising mist and flickering lights, and to have heard footsteps and the breaking of glass in this pub.

The pub was constructed as two cottages in the seventeenth century, although subsequent additions include bay windows from 1785 and a mid-nineteenth-century staircase.

The grade II listed building is one of the oldest in the city and used to have an attached stables for up to sixty-five horses.

E. MICKLEGATE BAR

This four-storey gatehouse on Micklegate gets its name from the Old Norse *mykla gata*, which meant 'great road', and was the ceremonial entrance for arriving monarchs.

In 1389, Richard II passed through the gate and touched the state sword, establishing this as a tradition for arriving royalty – at least six reigning monarchs have passed through the gate. In the medieval period the touch of a ruling monarch was said to have mystical powers, healing the sick and bestowing good luck.

With the lower part built in the twelfth century, its imposing stature was put to a grisly use when traitors' heads were displayed and left to rot and intimidate oncoming attackers.

The street runs from the east to what was once the southern entrance to the city; it was originally part of the Roman road to Tadcaster. Buildings along the road would have included the houses of wealthy citizens, small shops and taverns; there are also four grade I listed buildings and three medieval churches here.

Number 114 on the street was the birthplace of J. A. Hansom, who invented the horse-drawn hansom cab. This cab replaced the hackney carriage, previously the most common vehicle for hire, with its introduction of mechanical meters to measure the applicable fares.

Micklegate Bar

F. JACOB'S WELL

Just off the main street, down Trinity Lane, this grade I listed house was built around 1474 as lodgings for the chantry priest at the nearby priory.

After several changes of use, including as offices for a stage-coach business, alterations in 1815 led to it briefly becoming a pub before it was converted into a parish room for the nearby church.

G. ST MARTIN-CUM-GREGORY'S CHURCH

Dating back to the eleventh century, this grade I listed parish church has seen numerous alterations including chapels in 1430 and a porch and tower from 1655.

Its name comes from the merger with St Gregory's Church in 1585, although neither remains active and the building is now a public hall.

H. RIVER OUSE

The sixth-longest river in the UK at 129 miles, it is a continuation of the River Ure. The Ure runs for 74 miles before joining the River Swale near Linton-on-Ouse, where the river officially changes name.

Its source is at the village of Great Ouseburn and it continues through a large, wide, flat plain that commonly floods during heavy rain.

I. OUSE BRIDGE

There has been a bridge here since Roman times, with the wooden bridge of the Vikings collapsing in 1154 under the weight of expectant crowds gathered to greet St William's return from exile.

It was replaced by a stone bridge in the late twelfth century and in 1367 the first public toilets in England were opened on the bridge – alongside a jail, chapel, houses and shops.

The buildings were removed by 1793 and the bridge was dismantled between 1810 and 1818 to enable the construction of the current bridge – which was completed in 1821.

Ouse Bridge

3. THE KINGS ARMS

The only surviving building on First Water Lane – one of the three medieval streets demolished when clearing the slums in 1852.

It was built in the early seventeenth century, most likely as a warehouse or custom house for the river trade before it was converted to a pub in 1795.

It was renamed the Ouse Bridge Inn from 1867 to 1973, after which it was granted grade II listed status. It is the most flooded pub in the country, with its riverside location flooding, on average, four times a year.

Despite efforts to add a flood door, the fixtures and fittings are easily dismantled to be stored upstairs, where all of the beer and electrical devices are also kept.

It is rumoured to have been the resting place for the bodies of executed criminals, before they were strung up on the nearby bridge.

J. WATER LANES

This collection of three streets was the main thoroughfare from Castlegate to the river in medieval York.

The long, narrow lanes featured ramshackle, jettied buildings that overhung the walkway. They became associated with extreme poverty, crime and immorality such as prostitution, muggings and murder.

They were known by several names from their construction in the twelfth century through to their demolition in 1851. Their demolition came after they had become notorious for their unsanitary conditions and being the origin of cholera outbreaks in the city.

K. YORK DUNGEON

This modern tourist attraction is a live interactive horror show loosely based on historical events and was opened in 1986 following the success of the London Dungeon.

It caused controversy in 2007 when it offered people who

had been issued antisocial behaviour orders (ASBOs) free entry for the weekend in an attempt to deter future crimes by demonstrating the severe way they would have been punished for their behaviour in medieval times.

Despite significant publicity, and wide condemnation, no one took up the offer of free tickets.

4. BLUE BOAR

Prior to the original pub's demolition in 1730, it was popular with Royalist soldiers and Roger Cottam, who was envoy to Henry VII during the siege of York.

The current building became an important coaching inn between Leeds, Hull and Barnard Castle.

Legend claims that the ghost of Dick Turpin haunts the pub, as his body was kept overnight in the cellars following his execution. Turpin was a highwayman, robbing people on the 200-mile stretch of road between London and York. His exploits were romanticised by Victorian novelist William Harrison Ainsworth. Nowadays, his story is well known among Gen Z as popular TV show *Horrible Histories* featured a song based on his life, sung by actor Mathew Baynton.

When we visited to film, I sat in the cellar next to the reconstructed coffin of Dick Turpin, but when the lights flickered I made a hasty exit.

L. PAVEMENT

Once the heart of commercial Jorvik during the Viking era, the area was first recorded as Marketshire in 1086, before being known as Pavement from around 1329.

It was a popular spot for public gatherings and was most likely one of the first roads in the city to be paved, hosting events like bull-baiting and the execution of Thomas Percy, the 7th Earl of Northumberland.

A market cross was erected in 1671 and existed until its demolition in 1887, when road upgrades led to it becoming more of a thoroughfare.

5. THE THREE TUNS

This wonky timber-framed building was likely to have been constructed in the sixteenth century and has been recorded as a pub since at least 1782.

It was heavily altered during the nineteenth century; more recent renovations uncovered a cache of gold and silver coins from medieval times.

M. THE SHAMBLES

This famous medieval street was once known as the Great Flesh Shambles due to the many butcher's shops here. In 1885 alone, a whopping thirty-one were operating in the small area.

Since shambles is also a term for an open-air slaughterhouse or meat market, it has been referred to as this since around the fourteenth century. The narrow street and the timber-framed buildings' jettied floors, which overhung the alley, probably kept the meat in the shade and therefore fresher for longer, and the natural slope of the road allowed the offal and blood that was thrown into the street to wash away.

Although similar in appearance to the slums of Water Lanes, it survived demolition and many of the buildings remain intact.

N. DIAGON ALLEY

The fictional London street is an economic hub in the Harry Potter books, and legend has it that it was inspired by York's Shambles. There is something magical about the area, with the tall buildings surrounding a narrow route, the uneven pavement, and the hustle and bustle of tourists and locals. Entry to the street is granted by tapping a brick in the rear courtyard of the Leaky Cauldron pub, but I wouldn't recommend tapping around any of the pubs in this book.

Despite the wizard-themed shops opening along the street, the connection has been denied by the author, J.K. Rowling. There is also a street in Edinburgh that locals point to as potential inspiration, a theory that may hold some water as Rowling lived there while she was writing much of the series.

6. YE OLDE SHAMBLES TAVERN

Located in a former butcher's, the rear seating area is in the old slaughterhouse. It has a resident poltergeist, who threw three packing boxes across the bar under the watch of CCTV in July 2019; there is plenty of footage of this online.

O. SHAMBLES MARKET

The large open space behind the butcher's shops of the Shambles used to be a collection of small buildings and narrow alleyways before they were demolished in the 1950s.

At the time, the main markets in Parliament Street and St Sampson's Square either closed or reduced their opening hours and the displaced vendors were offered spots here, in the newly named Newgate Market. It was refurbished in 2014, at a cost of over £1.6 million, and renamed Shambles Market after the adjacent street.

The oldest of the stalls include the fishmonger's, Cross of York (opened in 1957), and Swain Family Butchers from 1972.

Shambles Market

7. THE MARKET CAT

Often referred to as the ugliest building in York, this three-storey 1960s corner pub was previously occupied by Yorkshire pawnbroker Herbert Brown & Son.

Given its previous use, the beer 'cellar' is unusually on the second floor, with views of the famous market.

P. GERT & HENRY'S

The oldest part of this timber-framed building on Jubbergate was constructed in the fourteenth century, then a second structure was erected in the seventeenth century, but over time the two have merged into a single property.

It had entered commercial use by 1830, first as a pharmacy, followed by an art shop, before becoming a hatter in 1870. Now a restaurant, it is one of the few buildings in the area that survived the creation of Shambles Market.

8. THE OLD WHITE SWAN

This timber-framed building was first used as an inn around 1703 and is one of the oldest pubs in the city. In the eighteenth century, part of the building was in the parish of Holy Trinity King's Court, and part in the Holy Trinity Goodramgate parish.

When both parishes claimed the right to charge a rent for the pub, the landlord painted a white line through the court-yard and kitchen and offered partial rent to each parish. In the early eighteenth century, brick extensions were added to either side of the original building, and used as a barber's shop, pigsty and hayloft.

The courtyard became the main entrance and although occasionally used for practical purposes such as the weekly poultry market, it is notable for hosting a showcase event introducing the world's tallest man, Patrick Cotter O'Brien, who was only the second man ever to be recorded as over 8 feet in height.

The inn became a starting point for several stagecoach routes, and the original mounting block can still be seen in the courtyard, as can a Roman column, underneath a glass panel in the pub's floor.

It's said that the pub is haunted by the ghosts of a group of Catholics who were captured while planning an escape to France, and they are said to rearrange chairs in a circle around a fire overnight.

Q. GOODRAMGATE

One of the original roads within the Roman walls of Eboracum, the street was first officially recorded in around 1180 in the parish of the Holy Trinity Church.

Despite several changes and developments – including the creation of a market in 1502 and road widening in 1771 – a few medieval buildings and pubs remain standing on the street.

THE SNICKLEWAY INN

This grade II* building has been known by many names since its construction in 1500 and its conversion to a pub during the eighteenth century.

It was originally named the Painters' Arms, before becoming the Square and Compasses, the Mason's Arms, the Board and the Joiner's Arms at various points.

Inside, the original sign from 1851, when it was called the Anglers Arms, hangs above the bar.

It was renamed the Snickleway Inn in 1994, in reference to the snickelways of York (see below) – but was deliberately misspelled to avoid copyright issues.

Reputedly the most haunted pub in York, regulars believe there to be five spirits, including Mrs Tulliver and her cat, Seamus; Marmaduke Buckle, a disabled man who took his own life while living in the property during the early eighteenth century; and an especially malevolent spirit who causes havoc in the cellars, which are accessed via a tiny hatch behind the bar.

The cellar of the Snickleway Inn is accessed by a tiny hatch behind the bar, which leads to a claustrophobic space that is said to be haunted.

9. THE HABIT

This small building with a roof terrace overlooking the cathedral was built in the sixteenth century and is in one of the oldest areas of the city.

Formerly a furniture shop, it was first used as a home for stonemasons and nearby monks.

R. THE SNICKELWAYS OF YORK

These narrow streets get their name from the portmanteau of snicket (meaning passageway between walls), ginnel (a narrow passageway through buildings) and alleyway, and was coined by local author Mark W. Jones in 1983 in his book of fifty walks within the city walls.

Jones's book is unusual as it was completely hand-written, despite several revised editions.

Many of the paths hold unusual names, such as Mad Alice Lane (named after an executed women who poisoned her husband), Mucky Peg Lane and Nether Hornpot Lane; the longest snickelway is 220 feet and the narrowest only 2 feet 7 inches wide.

10. THE ROYAL OAK

This former coaching inn dates to the fifteenth century, although it is rumoured to have been the site of a building as far back as the Viking occupation. The mock-Tudor frontage was installed around 1934.

It is reputedly haunted by several ghosts. Notably, a former sex worker in the front bar; ghostly children playing by the fire; and a tall, gaunt man in the back room. Upstairs, two female ghosts stalk the rooms: Alice is on the first floor and Mary lives in the flat at the top.

S. YORK MINSTER

The first record of a church on this site is from 627. The Anglican cathedral is the seat of the third-highest office in the Church of England, the Archbishop of York. Much of the Gothic building was constructed over 250 years between 1220 and 1472.

The east window, depicting the Last Judgement, is the largest piece of medieval stained glass in the world. The cathedral suffered serious damage and looting during the reign of Elizabeth I, in a concerted effort to remove Catholicism from the city.

However, the most destructive event in the building's history was a fire in 1984, which resulted in a total of 114 firefighters deliberately collapsing the roof with tens of thousands of gallons of water in order to save the rest of the building from destruction.

A subsequent investigation found it was probably caused by a lightning strike that sparked an electrical box on the roof.

Some traditionalists have suggested it was a sign from God of his displeasure at the consecration of David Jenkins – a bishop who went on to become one of the first clerics to participate in the public blessing of a civil partnership between two men (one of whom was a priest).

T. CONSTANTINE THE GREAT

The bronze statue, outside the minster, was erected in 1998 to commemorate the accession of Constantine as Roman emperor in AD 306, after the death of his father, Constantius Chlorus, in York. A bit late, but it's the thought that counts.

Constantine ruled until 337 and, as the first emperor to convert to Christianity, he played an important role in decriminalising the practice of Christianity, ceasing persecution and elevating the status of Christians in the Roman Empire.

U. ROMAN COLUMN

Discovered during an excavation of York Minster in 1969, the 25-foot column, made of magnesian limestone and millstone grit was relocated to the front of the school in Minster Yard.

It is believed to have been constructed in the first century and used as one of sixteen free-standing columns that supported the wall of the basilica on the site.

V. STONEGATE

First named in 1119, the street was originally populated by glass painters and goldsmiths, before being overtaken by bookshops and printers in the 1500s.

Given its proximity to the cathedral, it has often been used for civic processions. It was pedestrianised in 1974 and has remained so ever since.

Gunpowder plotter Guy Fawkes was born in the street in 1570 to Spanish immigrants, and he lived there until moving to London to pursue his political goals.

Now a popular tourist destination, most of the buildings are listed and include 54, 56 and 58 Stonegate, an impressive fourteenth-century timber-framed terrace; the twelfth-century Norman House, the oldest residence in the city; and several structures from the fifteenth century.

11. YE OLDE STARRE INNE

First licensed in 1644, the year of the siege of York by the Roundheads, the pub holds the longest continuous licence of any pub in York, and stakes claims to be the oldest in the country.

The sign for the pub hangs across the street, after then landlord Thomas Bulman signed an agreement with the owners of two shops on Stonegate that he could attach a sign to their premises in 1733.

Originally, the large stable-yard at the front of the pub faced the road, but this was filled in by new buildings, leaving the only access via a narrow alleyway. This meant nobody could see the pub, and patronage plummeted. The sign was moved in an effort to advertise the pub's entrance, and was luckily such a success that we can still enjoy Ye Olde Starre Inne hundreds of years later.

The well, in the small courtyard at the front of the pub, was probably the only source of fresh water in the area at the time.

Notable residents include the ghost of a Royalist officer from 1644, complete with a beaver hat, doublet and smart breeches; two black cats that may have been buried alive, behind the bar; and an old lady on the stairs.

Occasionally the blood-curdling screams of injured and dying soldiers can be heard coming up from the depths of the cellar. The space may have been used as an impromptu hospital during any one of the dozens of battles York has seen.

12. THE HOUSE OF THE TREMBLING MADNESS

This medieval-themed alehouse is filled with stuffed animal heads and was originally part of a Norman house, dating back to 1180.

It is easy to miss this pub, which was one of the most recommended to me in York, as the ancient room is actually above a crammed bottle shop filled with hundreds of different craft ales and beers.

13. THE PUNCH BOWL

Founded in 1675 as a coffee house, it became a pub in 1761 and gets its name from the Whigs – the political party that succeeded the Roundheads – who preferred to drink punch.

Since the Conservatives preferred to drink claret wine, the display of a punchbowl was deemed to be in support of the liberals. In its early years, the pub was the headquarters of the York Race Committee, and it was also popular with the bell-ringers at York Minster – a bell clapper has been used as a support in the rear bar since 1765.

It was granted grade II listed status in 1954, despite being the third iteration of the building following a series of devastating fires, with the last in 1930.

It was a lot of fun filming the York route for our social media, and after a rain-soaked day Maddie and I had earned our drinks.

MANCHESTER
(Salford to City)

Starting in the city of Salford, this route traces the outside ring road before heading over the river, past the iconic cathedral and down along the famous Deansgate before ending up in the busy canal basin.

As well as featuring two of Manchester's most famous pubs, the walk includes the iconic town hall, the Midland Hotel and the Central Library.

There is a huge variety of pubs along the route, which showcases some of the best that Manchester has to offer.

What I love about this route is that it starts seemingly some distance from the city centre and yet everything is so walkable.

Start from Salford Central station (M3 5ET).

1. **The Kings Arms (open from 4 p.m. Mon–Wed)** *1.30 p.m.*
11 Bloom Street, M3 6AN

2. **The Black Friar** *2.00 p.m.*
41–43 Blackfriars Road, M3 7DB

3. **Eagle Inn** *3.00 p.m.*
19 Collier Street, M3 7DW

4. **Mitre Hotel** *3.45 p.m.*
Shambles Square, 1–3 Cathedral Gates, M3 1SW

5. **The Old Wellington** *4.15 p.m.*
4 Cathedral Gates, M3 1SW

6. **The Old Nags Head** *5.00 p.m.*
19 Jackson's Row, M2 5WD

7. **The Temple** *5.45 p.m.*
100 Great Bridgewater Street, M1 5JW

8. **Peveril of the Peak** *6.30 p.m.*
127 Great Bridgewater Street, M1 5JQ

9. **The Britons Protection** *7.15 p.m.*
50 Great Bridgewater Street, M1 5LE

10. **The Wharf** *8.00 p.m.*
6 Slate Wharf, M15 4ST

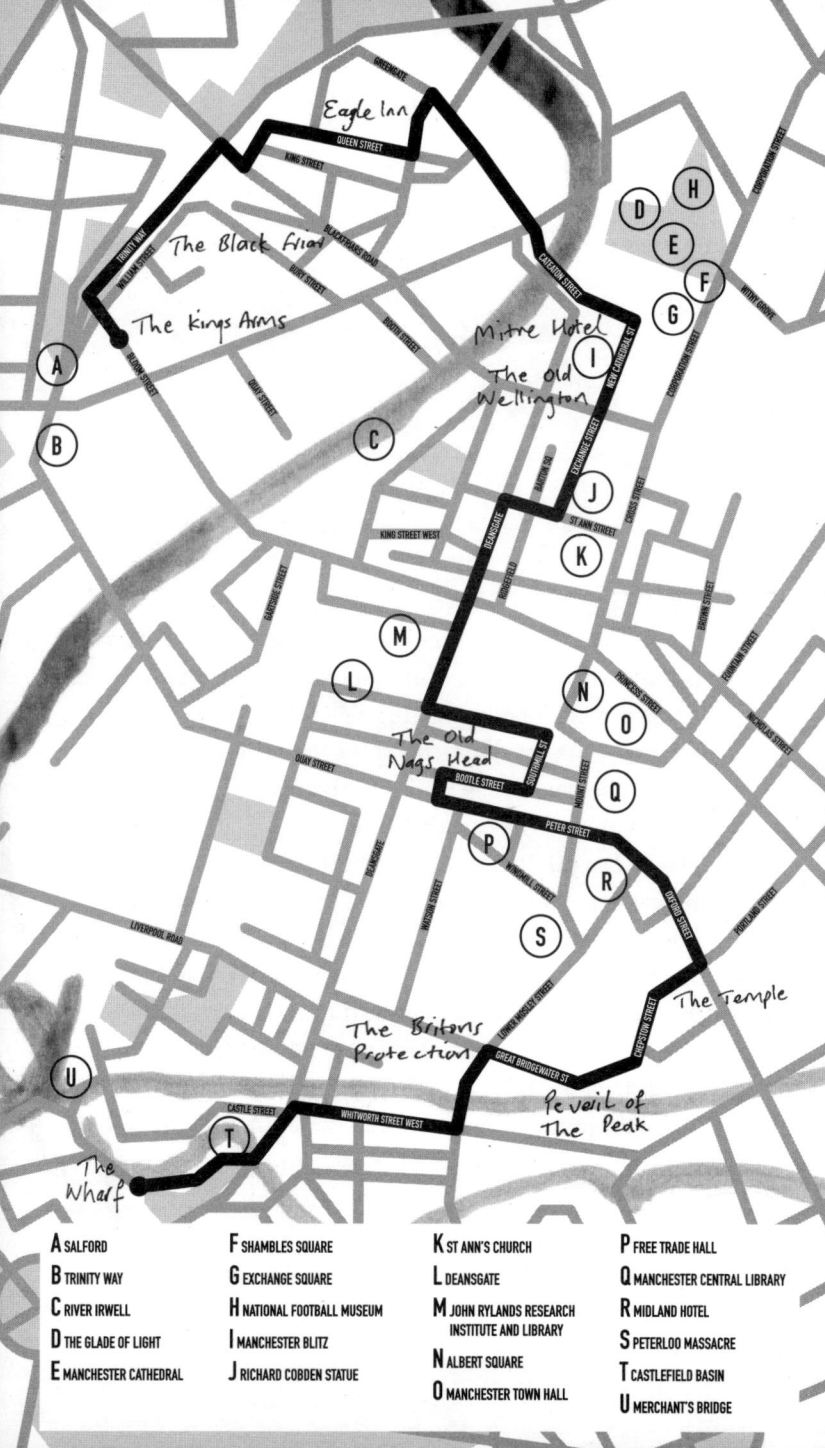

A SALFORD	**F** SHAMBLES SQUARE	**K** ST ANN'S CHURCH	**P** FREE TRADE HALL
B TRINITY WAY	**G** EXCHANGE SQUARE	**L** DEANSGATE	**Q** MANCHESTER CENTRAL LIBRARY
C RIVER IRWELL	**H** NATIONAL FOOTBALL MUSEUM	**M** JOHN RYLANDS RESEARCH INSTITUTE AND LIBRARY	**R** MIDLAND HOTEL
D THE GLADE OF LIGHT	**I** MANCHESTER BLITZ	**N** ALBERT SQUARE	**S** PETERLOO MASSACRE
E MANCHESTER CATHEDRAL	**J** RICHARD COBDEN STATUE	**O** MANCHESTER TOWN HALL	**T** CASTLEFIELD BASIN
			U MERCHANT'S BRIDGE

DIRECTIONS

Turn left out of the station, where **The Kings Arms (1, A)** is on the corner. Left out of the pub, before turning right on the main road, Trinity Way **(B)**, where **The Black Friar (2)** is dwarfed by the developments at the first major junction.

Take the small road opposite the pub, to the right, and follow it around the corner before a first left up Collier Street to **Eagle Inn (3)**. Retrace to Queen Street, turn left and follow the road past the car park, bearing right onto Greengate and underneath the railway tracks, before crossing the River Irwell **(C)** where the Glade of Light **(D)** is to the left behind Manchester Cathedral **(E)**. Follow Cateaton Street past **The Mitre Hotel (4)** on the corner of Shambles Square **(F)** which is occupied by **The Old Wellington (5)**.

Past the pub, before Exchange Square **(G)**, with the National Football Museum **(H)** further away, head down New Cathedral Street **(I)** before turning right at Saint Ann's Church **(J, K)** at the end of the pedestrian area.

Turn left onto Deansgate **(L)** past the John Rylands Research Institute and Library **(M)** where **The Old Nags Head (6)** is on the left along Jackson's Row.

Leave the rear of the pub and follow the road right, before Albert Square **(N, O)** before turning left at the main road at Free Trade Hall **(P)** heading past Manchester Central Library **(Q)** opposite the Midland Hotel **(R)**. **The Temple (7)** is on the right down the steps to a Victorian toilet block in the pedestrianised area.

Continue past the pub to the main road, where **Peveril of the Peak (8)** is on the main road, with **The Britons Protection (9, S)** a short walk further along the road.

Turn left from the pub and cross the canal, before turning right on the canal towpath, which comes out at the Castlefield Basin **(T)**. Cross the white Merchant's Bridge **(U)** to **The Wharf (10)**.

---

1. THE KINGS ARMS

First licensed in 1807, when it stood on the opposite side of the road, this pub moved into a larger location in the late 1800s. The current building started life as one of the three main local buildings alongside the gas company offices and Salford House.

The pub has been a popular meeting place for several clubs over the years, including the North of England Irish Terrier Club, founded in 1906; the Salford Friendly Anglers Society, the oldest angling society in the world; and the Knitting Club, whose members meet in the snug.

In 2011 it was taken over by Paul Heaton from the Beautiful South and his partner, Zena Barrie, and the pub has featured in TV shows *Fresh Meat*, *The Hairy Bikers* and *The Les Dawson Story*.

The stained-glass window was replaced with a replica in order for Robbie Coltrane to be thrown through it in an episode of the 1990s drama *Cracker*.

A. SALFORD

A cathedral city within the county of Greater Manchester, its granting of a market charter in 1230 made it initially much more culturally and commercially impactful than the adjoining Manchester and it was not until the Industrial Revolution of the later eighteenth century that their order of importance was reversed.

Between 2004 and 2013 the area around Salford Quays was extensively redeveloped as Media City, which now houses BBC studios, ITV and the set of *Coronation Street*.

The BBC remains the main occupier, having relocated more than 1,800 jobs as part of the closure of Birmingham's Pebble Mill Studios and the downsizing of its London sites.

B. TRINITY WAY

The final section of the Manchester and Salford Inner Relief Route (also known as the Manchester Inner Ring Road) was opened in 2004 as part of a planned series of roads. The aim was to ease congestion on Deansgate, although local opinions are divided on how successful this was.

2. THE BLACK FRIAR

Constructed in 1886, the building lay closed in a state of disrepair for many years before reopening in 2021 among the high rises, on the corner of a busy road.

Legend tells of a Benedictine monk, Benedict Farcire, who wandered across Europe sharing magical healing powers. He was known as the Black Friar, likely because of the colour of his robes.

When he reached Salford in 1886 it is said that his wandering days ceased and he opened this now grade II listed pub, which now has a large beer garden and modern restaurant.

Known amongst friends for his chameleonic 'Find Fize' game, it's almost impossible to spot The Sultan.

3. EAGLE INN

Once a Victorian terraced house, built around 1902, this grade II listed building features two symmetrical front bays in an Edwardian baroque style. Over recent years it has been refurbished to provide practice rooms for local musicians.

It was formerly known as the Old Lamp Oil and features a

distinctive terracotta plaque and ornate eagle above the front door.

The tiny beer garden to the rear is almost completely filled with a ping-pong table. However, my best hand-eye coordination usually involves raising a pint glass to my mouth.

C. RIVER IRWELL

A tributary of the River Mersey, it marks the boundary of Manchester and Salford, with the lower parts forming a section of the Manchester Ship Canal, which opened in 1896.

The developments were crucial to the area during the Industrial Revolution as the canal created a major inland seaport that led to the expansion of Trafford Park into Europe's largest industrial estate.

D. THE GLADE OF LIGHT

Opened to the public in 2022, this memorial commemorates the victims of the Manchester Arena bombing. The stone centrepiece incorporates personal memory capsules and is inscribed with the names of the twenty-two people who lost their lives when two bombers targeted an Ariana Grande concert in 2017.

The resulting explosion injured more than a thousand people and was the deadliest act of terrorism in the UK since the London bombings of 2005. Many of the victims were children, and since then Manchester and Grande have hosted multiple fundraisers for the people impacted and their families.

E. MANCHESTER CATHEDRAL

One of fifteen grade I listed buildings in Manchester, this former parish church was rebuilt multiple times between 1421 and 1882 in Perpendicular Gothic style, and became the cathedral for the Diocese of Manchester in 1847.

During the Christmas Blitz of 1940, all the stained-glass windows were blown out and the elaborate nineteenth-century organ was destroyed. The decision was made to install new designs, rather than try to recreate the ones that were destroyed, leading to the distinctive abstract art that can be seen today.

The release of the video game *Resistance: Fall of Man* in 2006 caused controversy due to the first-person shooter's unauthorised depiction of the cathedral and the use of weapons in the building.

Manchester Cathedral

4. THE MITRE HOTEL

The grade II listed building is a mix of sandstone and Jacobean architecture, and this corner pub overlooks Exchange Square. Built in 1815 as the Old Church Tavern, it is one of the oldest hotels in Manchester city centre.

Despite the recent refurbishments it still features much of its original charm – including a ghost that is said to walk the corridors. It was here that the then Prince Charles Stuart gathered his troops in 1745 ahead of the Battle of Prestonpans.

The ornate columns and arched windows are even more remarkable given they escaped unscathed from both the Blitz of 1940 and the IRA bombing in 1996.

F. SHAMBLES SQUARE

This medieval-style square was created in 1999 when the Old Wellington and Sinclair's Oyster Bar were relocated from the Old Shambles as part of major building work, following the IRA bombing in 1996.

The name is linked to the Middle English word *schamel*, meaning a bench for displaying meat. Throughout England there are several cities, such as York and Worcester, where old streets occupied by several butcher's shops are named shambles.

The current use of the word, which means disorder, has its origin in the disorganised alleyways where the open gutters would overspill with cuts of meat, offal and blood.

Shambles Square

5. THE OLD WELLINGTON

Built in 1552, the half-timbered Old Wellington is the oldest building of its kind in Manchester. It was once home to Manchester commerce, including the people behind the city's first bank, and the lucrative cotton industry.

It then became part of a draper's shop and the poet John Byrom was born in 1692 in the first-floor accommodation. Over time the building expanded to add a third storey and by 1830 it had been granted a licence where it was known as the Vintners Arms before changing to the Kenyon Vaults.

When it became known as the Wellington Inn, the upper floors were used by manufacturers of mathematical and optical equipment as well as a fishing tackle shop.

Many of the adjacent buildings were demolished to accommodate Victorian era developments, which were in turn destroyed during the Blitz in World War II.

Now it is the only surviving Tudor building in Manchester city centre; it was placed onto a concrete raft in 1971, to support its uneven walls.

After the IRA bombing in 1996, and the subsequent repair works, it was completely dismantled and rebuilt 980 feet from its original location.

G. EXCHANGE SQUARE

Created as part of the redevelopments after 1996, the area has become a major shopping destination, with the relocation of two pubs allowing for the opening of a large Marks & Spencer store.

It also housed the Wheel of Manchester, which was a Ferris

wheel that was erected in 2004, then dismantled just three years later. Originally intended to be a temporary structure, a replacement was installed almost immediately, before a larger (still unconstructed) version was planned in 2010.

H. NATIONAL FOOTBALL MUSEUM

Originally based in Deepdale, the home of founding Football League member Preston North End and the oldest continuously used football stadium in the world, the museum was moved to Manchester in 2012.

After securing National Lottery funding in 1997, a groundbreaking ceremony was held, with FIFA president Sepp Blatter as a guest of honour. Despite attracting more than 100,000 visitors each year, it struggled with funding, as costs continuously outweighed incoming funds.

Although the then chairman of the Football League, Brian Mawhinney, had suggested relocating to Wembley, in 2009 Manchester City Council offered a package to secure its longterm future in the city.

Among the 140,000 collected items, of which around 2,500 are on display at any one time, are both balls used in the first World Cup final in 1930; the ball from England's only World Cup triumph in 1966; and the original rules of association football that were written down when the Football Association was formed in the Freemasons' Tavern in London, in 1863.

I. MANCHESTER BLITZ

As the location of an important inland port and as a major industrial city at the heart of war production, the entire area was severely damaged in air raids between 1940 and 1942. German Luftwaffe planes would fly in at night, dropping bombs in an attempt to destroy the infrastructure of the city, slowing shipments of weapons to Allied forces on the front lines.

The heaviest raids occurred in the days leading up to Christmas 1940, with nearly seven hundred people killed and more than two thousand injured. Neighbouring Salford and Stretford were also damaged, with a major loss of life, and the cathedral, Royal Exchange, Free Trade Hall and assize courts were damaged as nearly 500 tons of explosives and two thousand incendiaries were dropped over two nights.

J. RICHARD COBDEN STATUE

A political pioneer and ardent campaigner for free trade and peace, Cobden was one of eleven children born in Sussex to poor farmers. To give him a better life, he was sent to live with his uncle in Yorkshire.

When he was fifteen, he moved to London where he became a travelling salesman of muslin and calico, eventually working his way to becoming the owner of a Manchester-based factory that generated up to £10,000 a year (equivalent to £745,000 today). Around this time, he turned his interests to politics, becoming one of Manchester's first elected aldermen.

By the time of his death, at sixty, in 1865 he had played a crucial role in the Anti-Corn Law League, lost his parliamentary seat while protesting against the Crimean War, and been named in the 1860 treaty that promoted closer free trade with France.

K. ST ANN'S CHURCH

Although named after Jesus's maternal grandmother, St Anne, the spelling pays tribute to Lady Bland (Ann) who was the patron of the church.

The foundation stone was laid in 1709, and the site was consecrated in 1712. It was constructed using locally sourced red Collyhurst sandstone which, due to is soft nature, has eroded and been replaced almost completely.

L. DEANSGATE

Named after the River Dene, it is one of Manchester's oldest roads, dating back to Roman times when it passed the fort of Mamucium on to the road to Chester.

It remained rural until around 1730, when riverside developments led to a population increase that, by the nineteenth century, saw its use split between shopping, office buildings and slums for the working class.

The long, straight road has hosted several events, including the launch of the now defunct A1 Grand Prix. Jenson Button drove his McLaren F1 along it, and the world's fastest man, Usain Bolt, set the 150-metres world record at the inaugural Great City Games. Bolt ran the distance in an impressive 14.35 seconds, beating the previous record set in 1983 by Italian sprinter Pietro Mennea.

M. JOHN RYLANDS RESEARCH INSTITUTE AND LIBRARY

Founded in memory of entrepreneur and philanthropist John Rylands, who was Manchester's first multi-millionaire and the owner of the UK's largest textile manufacturer, which employed more than 15,000 workers in seventeen mills.

When it was opened to the public in 1900, the area was occupied by tall warehouses, derelict buildings and narrow streets. Despite being a popular and fashionable part of the city, the plot of land was an awkward shape for such a large neo-Gothic construction.

It was one of the first buildings in Manchester to be lit by electricity, which was generated on-site until 1950, as well as boasting a complex ventilation system to protect the library's books and manuscripts from smoke or chemical damage.

Upon opening it contained around 70,000 books, and the collection has since grown to include several notable volumes, including a first edition of James Joyce's *Ulysses*.

Its special collections contain a Gutenberg Bible (the first mass-printed book in Europe); the most extensive collection of the Aldine Press editions of classical works from Venice; and possibly the earliest extant record of part of the New Testament – St John's fragment from around AD 125–175.

6. THE OLD NAGS HEAD

This Victorian pub was a regular haunt of George Best, and it has a huge collection of pictures of the football star, as well as other Manchester United players.

The roof garden features a mural celebrating some of the

region's most iconic artists – Noel Gallagher, Johnny Marr, Morrissey, Steve Coogan, Frank Sidebottom and Maxine Peake – and a chimney dedicated to Tony Wilson.

Because of the proximity of their headquarters at the time, it was a popular hangout for police officers in the 1960s.

N. ALBERT SQUARE

The square was repurposed from once derelict land as a memorial following the death of Prince Albert in 1861 and completed three years later. He died of typhoid, leaving Queen Victoria a grieving widow.

Despite the ongoing cotton famine, the project received significant public support; people donated more than £6,000, and the Manchester Unity of Bricklayers provided more than 50,000 bricks. More than a hundred buildings were demolished on the land, and it was decided to relocate the council offices to a larger, purpose-built town hall on the square.

The square contains several monuments to the likes of banker Oliver Heywood; John Bright, the radical who promoted free trade; the former bishop of Manchester James Fraser; and former prime minister William Gladstone. The largest statue is of Prince Albert.

O. MANCHESTER TOWN HALL

Designed by famed architect Alfred Waterhouse, whose Gothic style is most famously seen in London's Natural History Museum. It was completed in 1877, and its imposing exterior is dominated by a 280-foot clock tower.

Although the building looks medieval in style, it was constructed with fireproof concrete and iron beams, and fitted with the latest nineteenth-century technologies such as gas lighting and a warm-air heating system.

Most council operations have now moved to the adjacent town hall extension that was constructed in 1927.

P. FREE TRADE HALL

Built on the site of the Peterloo Massacre, the building was constructed between 1853 and 1856 in recognition of the repeal of the Corn Laws in 1846, which marked a decisive shift towards free trade in the UK.

Charles Dickens performed in the hall in 1857; Benjamin Disraeli delivered his 'One Nation' speech in 1872; and Winston Churchill defended Britain's free trade policy in 1904.

It was also the location of Bob Dylan's infamous concert in 1966 when an audience member shouted 'Judas!' at Dylan for switching from an acoustic to an electric guitar.

Q. MANCHESTER CENTRAL LIBRARY

After the passing of the Public Libraries Act of 1850, Manchester was the first local authority to provide a library, which opened in Campfield during 1852 at a ceremony attended by Charles Dickens.

When the premises declined, the library was moved in 1877; a the new building was designed in 1926 and opened in 1934 by King George V.

The author of *A Clockwork Orange*, Anthony Burgess, was a regular visitor and his autobiography recounts being seduced by an older woman who he met at the indexing area.

R. MIDLAND HOTEL

Opened in 1903, this grand station hotel was built to serve passengers of the Midland Railway heading to or from St Pancras in London. It cost a staggering £1 million and included a thousand-seat purpose-built theatre to entertain the 70,000 guests that stayed in its first year.

Luxury car and aeroplane-engine manufacturing company Rolls-Royce was founded in 1904, shortly after a meeting at the hotel between engineers Charles Rolls and Henry Royce. Legend claims that Adolf Hitler coveted the hotel as a potential Nazi headquarters in Britain, and much of the surrounding area was spared during bombing raids in World War II.

Its restaurant, the French, was awarded one of the UK's first Michelin stars, in 1974; a few years earlier, the 'inappropriately dressed' Beatles had been refused entry.

7. THE TEMPLE

This former Victorian underground toilet block is referenced in Elbow's song 'Grounds for Divorce' by frontman and Mancunian Guy Garvey.

Although there has been some restoration, many of the original tiles and railings remain, with graffiti going back to the 1800s.

8. PEVERIL OF THE PEAK

This pub is run by the city's longest-serving landlady, Nancy Swanick – she's been there for fifty-four years as of 2025. A commemorative mirror celebrating her first forty years hangs over the fireplace in the snug.

It was built around 1820, but much of the exterior was remodelled around 1900, and what would have been the original terrace has been demolished as the building has been surrounded by office blocks and apartments.

Although the origin of the name is uncertain, one theory is that it comes from an 1823 novel by Sir Walter Scott, while others point to a stagecoach that travelled between London and Manchester in just two days.

One of the most distinctive exteriors, but inside is also a treasure-trove of memorabilia.

9. THE BRITONS PROTECTION

Famous for its ornate interior, this two-hundred-year-old pub features 1930s urinals and a serving hatch behind the bar. Its name stems from its use as an army recruiting venue. There are military murals and references throughout, and it is one of only three city-centre buildings that stood near the site of the Peterloo Massacre of 1819.

During the Napoleonic Wars of 1803–15 it was a refuge for locals, who hid from recruiters in the basement and tunnels below. Forced enlistment was not uncommon at the time, so young men often refused to go anywhere without a quick escape route.

Rumours persist that the once-classified nuclear war tunnels under the city can be accessed through the cellars; the underground network was built in 1954 – 115 feet below the city streets – but only publicly acknowledged in 1968.

S. PETERLOO MASSACRE

Following the end of the Napoleonic Wars in 1815, Britain fell into an economic slump, worsened by the Corn Laws, which led to massive unemployment and a poor harvest. The Corn Laws were a series of trade restrictions and tariffs placed on imported grain, making bread and other food staples ridiculously expensive.

During this time of unrest only 11 per cent of adult males had the right to vote, with even fewer eligible in the worst-hit areas of the industrial north of England. Women were not allowed to vote at all, meaning only around 5 per cent of the population were making the decisions for everybody. Encouraged by the Radical political movement, huge crowds gathered in the north-west to protest against the rejection of parliamentary petitions proposing change.

On 16 August 1819, Henry Hunt addressed a mass rally, organised by the Manchester Patriotic Union on St Peter's Field. The local yeomanry tried to apprehend Hunt, a woman was knocked down and a child was killed, then the 15th Hussars cavalry regiment charged the crowd, causing panic and injuring between four hundred and seven hundred protestors.

In an ironic reference to the Battle of Waterloo, the incident was nicknamed the Peterloo Massacre by the radical *Manchester Observer* newspaper.

It is widely considered one of the defining political moments of its time, and the public were horrified by the carnage as mounted infantry attacked an otherwise peaceful protest.

For several months afterwards, the authorities believed that the country was heading towards an armed rebellion; there were attempted uprisings in Huddersfield and Burnley as well as a foiled plot to assassinate the cabinet at a dinner.

Passing legislation to supress uprisings, capturing and arresting every significant radical reformer and creating a central police force – London's Metropolitan Police – reduced civil liberties to a lower standard than before the massacre.

T. CASTLEFIELD BASIN

Originally the site of the Roman fort, Mamucium, which was guarded by a cohort of approximately five hundred stationed troops in AD 79; by the time the Romans withdrew in 410, it had doubled in size.

The current function of the area began in 1764, when the Bridgewater Canal – the world's first industrial canal – terminated here. The canal was built to transport large amounts of coal from the Duke of Bridgewater's mine in Worsley into the city centre.

The project to complete the canal nearly bankrupted the duke, who acquired a £25,000 loan (£4 million in 2025), but the successful completion – a significant moment at the start of the Industrial Revolution – earned him over £80,000 each year and he became one of richest men in England.

U. MERCHANT'S BRIDGE

Built in 1996, the bridge is wider at its centre, allowing pedestrians to stop and admire the view over the basin.

10. THE WHARF

Although the first wharf on the canal junction was constructed around 1779, the current structure was erected in 1998 on the site of two commercial buildings.

Purpose-built as a pub, it was originally called Jackson's Wharf before it ceased trading in 2005. Following the regeneration of the nearby Trafford Centre and Media City, developers planned to tear down much of the area to create a huge apartment block complex, but widespread negative reaction halted future plans.

These days the terrace is a wonderful place to grab a beer on a sunny day.

I've got to meet many interesting personalities on the crawls, and few things can be as funny as a few beers with a famous comedian like Eshaan, who tours all around the UK.

MANCHESTER
(Victoria to Piccadilly)

Starting at the Northern Quarter, the route winds through some of the oldest parts of the city and the areas that have seen significant regeneration efforts.

It's hard to believe that some of the pubs not only still exist but continue to thrive despite the modern developments.

While retaining its music and fashion heritage, the route also passes the famous 'Animal Run' before heading past one of the largest Chinatown districts in the UK and down into the Gay Village.

With a wide variety of pubs, the journey concludes in one of Manchester's most iconic music venues in the developed Piccadilly area.

Start from Manchester Victoria station (M99 1ZW).

1. **The Angel** *1.30 p.m.*
6 Angel Street, M4 4BQ

2. **The Marble Arch Inn** *2.00 p.m.*
73 Rochdale Road, M4 4HY

3. **The Crown & Kettle** *3.00 p.m.*
2 Oldham Road, M4 5FE

4. **Castle Hotel** *3.30 p.m.*
66 Oldham Street, M4 1LE

5. **The Rat & Pigeon** *4.15 p.m.*
33 Back Piccadilly, M1 1HP

6. **The Bank** *5.00 p.m.*
57 Mosley Street, M2 3FF

7. **Grey Horse Inn** *5.30 p.m.*
80 Portland Street, M1 4QX

8. **Circus Tavern** *6.00 p.m.*
86 Portland Street, M1 4GX

9. **The Molly House** *6.30 p.m.*
26 Richmond Street, M1 3NB

10. **The Bulls Head** *7.15 p.m.*
84 London Road, M1 2PN

11. **Star and Garter** *8.00 p.m.*
18–20 Fairfield Street, M1 2QF

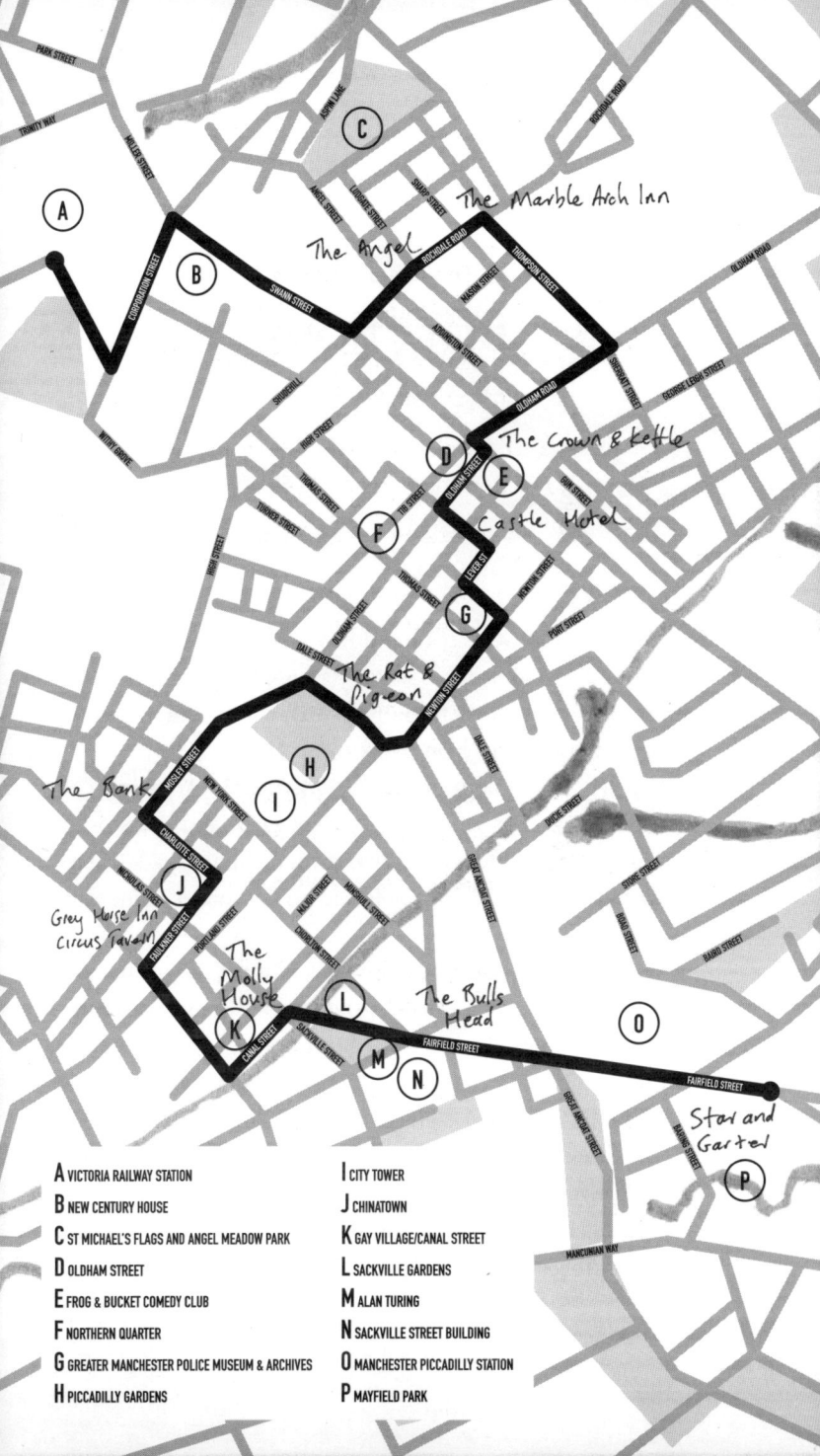

The Marble Arch Inn

The Angel

The Crown & Kettle

Castle Hotel

The Rat & Pigeon

The Bank

Grey Horse Inn
Circus Tavern

The Molly House

The Bulls Head

Star and Garter

A VICTORIA RAILWAY STATION

B NEW CENTURY HOUSE

C ST MICHAEL'S FLAGS AND ANGEL MEADOW PARK

D OLDHAM STREET

E FROG & BUCKET COMEDY CLUB

F NORTHERN QUARTER

G GREATER MANCHESTER POLICE MUSEUM & ARCHIVES

H PICCADILLY GARDENS

I CITY TOWER

J CHINATOWN

K GAY VILLAGE/CANAL STREET

L SACKVILLE GARDENS

M ALAN TURING

N SACKVILLE STREET BUILDING

O MANCHESTER PICCADILLY STATION

P MAYFIELD PARK

DIRECTIONS

Leave the station **(A)**, turn left down Corporation Street and cross the ring road at New Century House **(B)** where the road curves right, past St Michael's Flags **(C)**, where **The Angel (1)** is at the end of the road on the corner.

Turn left from the pub, where **The Marble Arch Inn (2)** is further up on the left. Retrace a few yards and cross onto Thompson Street before turning right at the main road, where **The Crown & Kettle (3)** can be found on the corner of the first busy junction.

Follow Oldham Street **(D)** opposite, past the Frog & Bucket **(E, F)** towards the **Castle Hotel (4)** on the left-hand side of the road. Take a few steps back and head down Warwick Street, turning right at Lever Street, then left on Faraday Street. At the main road turn right to pass the Police Museum **(G)** before taking the fifth right, onto Back Piccadilly, where **The Rat & Pigeon (5)** is on the next corner.

Turn right from the pub and then left at the first junction, before heading over Piccadilly Gardens **(H, I)** to the right-hand corner opposite, then down Mosley Street, until you come to **The Bank (6)**.

Head down Charlotte Street adjacent to the pub before crossing and turning right down Faulkner Street and through Chinatown **(J)** then turn left before the arch, where, after turning right again at the main road, there is **Grey Horse Inn (7)**, with **Circus Tavern (8)** a couple of doors down. Exit past the pub and turn left at the first junction, before turning left at Canal Street **(K)** and following the water, before a short left then right at the first bridge where the mural on the side of **The Molly House (9)** is obvious.

Retrace the route, back over the bridge and through Sackville Gardens **(L, M, N)** before turning left and following the main road as it curves right, all the way to **The Bulls Head (10)** at the junction. Continue over the road alongside the station **(O)** until reaching **The Star and Garter (11)** in front of Mayfield Park **(P)**.

A. VICTORIA RAILWAY STATION

The second busiest Manchester station (after Piccadilly) it opened in 1844 and serves as the main terminus for services to and from northern England. After being voted the worst major regional interchange station in 2009, it underwent extensive modernisation, which was completed in 2015 at a cost of £44 million.

The entrance features a large, white tiled map that shows

the former network of the Lancashire and Yorkshire Railway, which was created from an amalgamation of several other networks around the station's opening.

The 2015 works restored parts of the concourse that had been derelict since suffering bomb damage in World War II, including the glass dome and mosaics of the first-class lounge (now a café), and the 1909 wood-panelled booking hall.

B. NEW CENTURY HOUSE

To most this is an unremarkable high-rise office block, built for the Co-operative Insurance Society in 1962, but it was grade II listed in 1995 as a fine example of a post-war office building – with some considering it to be one of the finest modernist towers in the UK.

It incorporates a thousand-seat hall, where Jimi Hendrix, Jerry Lee Lewis, the Kinks, Procol Harum and local stars the Hollies played in the 1960s. In the 1980s it became a legendary venue for the all-night acid house parties of the Madchester era.

C. ST MICHAEL'S FLAGS AND ANGEL MEADOW PARK

At the heart of a once affluent suburb, poverty and disease during the Industrial Revolution of the nineteenth century caused the area to decline.

The church in the park, built in 1788, was dubbed by locals the ugliest in Manchester. It appears in several paintings by local artist L. S. Lowry.

The surrounding area become the city's largest cemetery.

Used as a common final resting place for the city's poorest people, it is estimated that more than 40,000 bodies were buried here, with the decline in living conditions leading to unscrupulous people digging up soil to sell as fertiliser.

Its name comes from the subsequent Burial Act of 1855, which enforced covering the graves with flagstones ('flags') to deter grave robbers. The area fell into further disrepute and became known for prostitution, cockfights and bare-knuckle contests in the second half of the nineteenth century.

The church closed in 1930 and was demolished five years later.

In 2004, over £200,000 was raised from grants and donations to re-landscape the area and install modern street furniture.

1. THE ANGEL

Part of a gaggle of pubs in the area in 1851, this is the only survivor; the Weaver's Arms has been demolished and the Brewer's Arms and George Inn are now car parks.

Previously a notorious slum area known as Angel Meadows, the area has seen significant development, with the construction of high-rise flats and hotels overlooking the busy junction of Rochdale Road.

2. THE MARBLE ARCH INN

Built in 1888 as a prestige project for McKenna's Brewery, on the site of an 1829 pub, it was fitted with electric lighting from the start. The building and its iconic façade were granted grade II listed status in 1998. Despite its name, the entrance is red granite.

Alterations in 1954 covered up the barrel-vaulted ceiling and decorative frieze, but they were exposed again in the 1980s.

In 1997 it was the birthplace of the Marble Brewery; a copper and hot liquor tank was installed at the back of the pub, although the brewery outgrew the premises in 2011 and moved to the railway arches on Williamson Street.

The sloped floor is said to often catch locals out; we tested the dip by rolling a can along the floor!

3. THE CROWN & KETTLE

This pub was opened around 1800, but there has been a building on this site as far back as 1734 – initially serving as a courthouse.

The Gothic structure was first called the Iron Dish and Cob of Coal before it was grade II listed in 1974.

Fire damage forced the pub to close in 1989, and it required significant restoration before reopening in 2005, with Historic England supporting the efforts to maintain the stone columns, which were once used to hold chandeliers from the ceiling roses.

Half of the pub's ceiling has been returned to its former glory, with the other showcasing the original installations. It is rumoured that the mahogany panelling in the snug was sourced from an airship.

D. OLDHAM STREET

Until the 1970s this street was Manchester's main shopping area, but the construction of the Arndale Centre mall saw many of the established stores relocate.

These days most businesses occupying the street are retro or vintage outlets, music stores or live music venues.

E. FROG & BUCKET COMEDY CLUB

This legendary venue was one of the first comedy clubs to open in the area, originally around the corner on Newton Street in 1994. Two years later it relocated to the current building, which was originally a bank. The reinforced structure protected it from the IRA bombing in 1996 and the club reopened just three days later.

Several comedy icons have performed at the pub over the years. It was here that John Bishop, after separating from his wife, wandered into an open mic night and got up on stage on a whim.

Other performers have included Jason Manford, Lee Mack, Johnny Vegas, Peter Kay and Jack Whitehall.

To celebrate their twenty-first birthday the owner, Dave Perkin, erected a memorial to all those who had 'died' on stage, and amateur nights encourage acts to compete to last at least five minutes before they are heckled off.

F. NORTHERN QUARTER

The area centred around Oldham Street was named the Northern Quarter as part of the developments and gentrification of the area during the 1990s.

While the area had some settlements as far back at the fourteenth century, it was not until the Industrial Revolution that the population expanded significantly. In the 1840s, when it became the textile capital of the world, it was a place of extreme wealth and extreme poverty.

The city rode the wave of its manufacturing success through the early twentieth century and reached its peak in 1912 when 8 billion square yards of material were produced and sold out of Manchester – earning it the nickname Cottonopolis. However, rising costs and cheaper international production led to a decline that saw many mills and factories close in the 1960s and 1970s.

4. CASTLE HOTEL

Originally opened as the Crown and Sceptre in 1776, the present name was chosen around the late nineteenth century. The glazed tile exterior was fitted in 1904 by Kay's Atlas Brewery and it was granted grade II listed status in 1988.

It fell into disrepair and was closed in 2008, before reopening a year later under the ownership of *Coronation Street* actor Rupert Hill and his business partner Jonny Booth. Despite its small frontage it hides a deceptively large live music hall.

G. GREATER MANCHESTER POLICE MUSEUM & ARCHIVES

The original home of the Manchester and Salford Police (and then the Greater Manchester Police) for a hundred years between 1879 and 1979.

It underwent extensive restoration to reflect Victorian policing and was reopened as a museum in 1981.

5. THE RAT & PIGEON

Operating as a public house since the 1870s, this corner pub was known as the Wellington before finding fame as the notorious Mother Mac's from 1969.

In 1976, then landlord Arthur Bradbury murdered his wife, their young daughter, his two stepsons and a cleaner before killing himself by setting the pub on fire.

After a period of disrepair and closure, it reopened under the current name in summer 2024.

It's a hard life jumping on the train to explore the country's pubs.

H. PICCADILLY GARDENS

Originally the site of the Royal Infirmary from 1755, and redeveloped in 1763 into the Royal Lunatic Asylum, the area had previously been occupied by water-filled clay pits known as daub holes.

In 1854 the holes were turned into important fountains, featuring figures such as the Duke of Wellington, Sir Robert

Peel and John Dalton. The hospital buildings were demolished by 1910.

Although the use of the site was uncertain for many years, it was eventually laid out as a sunken garden between the 1930s and 1950s after the council decided not to build in the open space. By the end of the twentieth century the area was increasingly unpopular, and a competition was held in 2021 to determine the future use of the space.

I. CITY TOWER

The second-tallest office building in Manchester, it was completed in 1965 and is the city's main broadcast transmission site for stations including Radio X, Capital FM and XS Manchester.

6. THE BANK

Despite its name, it was originally built as the Portico Library (which still survives upstairs) before becoming a pub in 1873 and taking its name from the Bank of Athens, which leased the property in 1921.

It was constructed in a Greek revival style, using Runcorn stone, by a group of local businessmen between 1803 and 1806, after their visit to a private members' club in Liverpool, the Athenaeum, inspired them to create a similar building at the heart of Manchester.

J. CHINATOWN

The second-largest Chinatown in the UK, the archway at its entrance was completed in 1987, long after the first Chinese settlers arrived in the early twentieth century.

The first Chinese restaurant in Manchester, Ping Hong, opened in 1948, but by the 1970s many other Chinese businesses had opened, including a government office and a branch of the Hong Kong and Shanghai Banking Corporation (more widely recognised these days as HSBC).

Manchester is twinned with Wuhan, which is commonly believed to have been the source of the Covid-19 pandemic.

Chinatown

7. GREY HORSE INN

This tiny building was a weaver's cottage before it was converted into a pub in 1851, with the upstairs floors retaining the original garret windows.

The one-room establishment was rumoured to be used

for clandestine meetings between British and Russian spies during the post-Cold War years.

The name of the pub, and others nearby, leads this stretch to be known as the Animal Run. Many of the animal-based names reportedly come from a travelling circus that used to stop in the area.

8. CIRCUS TAVERN

Claiming to be the smallest bar in Europe, the building dates to 1790 but it didn't become a pub until 1842, when it was taken over by a brewery.

The front room is filled with memorabilia showcasing local history and entertainers, while the back room focuses on football memorabilia; Manchester United legend George Best regularly propped up this tiny bar.

K. GAY VILLAGE/CANAL STREET

Although the street was developed during the construction of the adjacent Rochdale Canal, it was not until the twentieth century that the area become associated with the gay community. Following the collapse of the cotton factories and the dereliction of the area, it became the perfect place for clandestine meetings among the dark and disused buildings.

After over a decade of clampdowns in the area, led by James Anderton (the chief constable of Greater Manchester Police) before his retirement in 1991, a gay bar called Manto was opened and became the first to feature windows to reveal what was happening in the bar.

Prior to this, it was common for establishments to hide

their activity, and for the first six months of Manto's existence it is claimed it lost money due to the patrons' reluctance to be caught inside by casual passers-by.

Following the passing of a number of non-discriminatory polices in the 1980s and 1990s, larger bars opened in the area, and it was brought to wider public attention as the setting for the TV series *Queer as Folk* in 1999.

9. THE MOLLY HOUSE

This pub is adorned with a striking mural featuring queer icons Emmeline Pankhurst, Alan Turing, and drag queens Foo Foo Lammar and Anna Phylactic.

The former tailor's shop opened as a bar in 2010 and gets its name from the eighteenth-century equivalent of a gay bar. They were particularly important as places where queer men – nicknamed 'mollies' – could meet without fear of prosecution – or, worse, castration or execution.

The iconic artwork on the side of the Molly House marks the start of Gay Village.

L. SACKVILLE GARDENS

This patch of green space was laid out in 1900 and contains several memorials including the *Beacon of Hope*, a column designed to celebrate and acknowledge people living with HIV/AIDS and to remember those who have lost their lives to the disease.

Also present, seated on a park bench, is a statue of Alan Turing, who was widely regarded as the 'father of modern computing'. Turing is depicted holding an apple, a symbol often used to represent forbidden love; it is also the fruit of the tree of knowledge and the object that inspired Isaac Newton's theory of gravity.

M. ALAN TURING

Born in Maida Vale, London, Turing was pivotal to the Allies' successful efforts in World War II. He led Britain's codebreaking department, Hut 8, at Bletchley Park, which cracked the sophisticated Enigma machine used by the Nazis. Historians believe that without Turing the war would have gone on far longer, and he may have saved 14–21 million lives.

After the war, he went on to design one of the first stored-program computers, but because his contributions were covered under the Official Secrets Act, he wasn't fully recognised during his lifetime. Without his work, modern computing as we know it today would not exist.

In 1952, Turing was prosecuted for homosexual acts and accepted chemical castration as an alternative to prison; he took his own life by cyanide poisoning just two years later, aged forty-one.

Following a 2009 campaign, the then British prime minister

Gordon Brown made an official public apology for 'the appalling way [he] was treated' and Queen Elizabeth II granted him a Royal Pardon four years later.

A 2017 law, often known as 'The Alan Turing Law', retroactively pardoned men cautioned or convicted under historical legislation that had outlawed homosexual acts at the time.

Alan Turing

N. SACKVILLE STREET BUILDING

This impressive French Renaissance-style building was constructed in 1902 and is largely occupied by the University of Manchester. The terracotta building was extended between 1927 and 1957, largely delayed due to the impact of the depression and World War II.

Original plans included a swimming pool installed on the top floor, but concerns that the excess weight could cause structural issues led to the cancellation of the project.

Celebrity steeplejack and television personality Fred Dibnah installed the steel reinforcement bands on the building's chimney.

10. THE BULLS HEAD

It has been suggested that a pub has been on this site since 1786, but it does not appear on town records before 1851, when it was next to the Wheatsheaf (which was subsequently demolished to make way for the new road layout).

O. MANCHESTER PICCADILLY STATION

With more than 32 million passengers at its peak, Piccadilly is the busiest station in Manchester and the third busiest in the UK outside London, behind Birmingham New Street and Leeds.

It was opened as Store Street station in 1842, renamed Manchester London Road five years later, and then Manchester Piccadilly in 1960, after the road and nearby gardens.

*Never a fan of beer in plastic –
almost every occasion ends in
a spillage.*

11. THE STAR AND GARTER

Constructed in 1803, it was moved brick-by-brick between 1849 and 1877 following the expansion of the adjacent train station. Initially built as a hotel, its name originated from the insignia belonging to the Order of the Garter – the most senior order of knighthood in the British honours system.

Because the nearby station was a major target of bombing raids during World War II, the building suffered significant damage to the roof. Given the proximity of Mayfield station, as well as Piccadilly, it regularly catered for both railway and post office workers.

Despite receiving grade II listed status in 1988, it fell into disrepair and the brewery closed it. The surrounding area became a red-light district, with numerous derelict buildings.

After reopening, under new owners, in 1991, the venue quickly developed a reputation as a live music venue and nightclub. It has been used as a filming location for TV shows such as *Prime Suspect*, *Cracker*, *The Body Farm* and *Brassic*.

P. MAYFIELD PARK

Opened in 2022, the first new public park in Manchester for over a century is named after the former train station and nearby industrial area.

The area had been largely derelict since the 1980s but is now the first phase of a development that will include more than 1,500 houses. During excavations the intact remains of two large tiled swimming pools, water heaters, flues and pumps were discovered intact, from the Mayfield Baths building, which was lost to history following its demolition after bomb damage sustained during World War II.

ACKNOWLEDGEMENTS

This book could not exist without the wonderful support of friends, family and, of course, all the great pubs and staff that serve our country.

I'm very appreciative of everyone who has followed me on social media and given me the confidence to compile further books. The most amazing times have been when I have seen people in pubs holding one of my books.

It has been incredibly hard to compile this book, in the knowledge that so many great pubs and locations will be missed out. We are lucky to have a great pub heritage, and to have built communities around public houses for hundreds of years; even today, in the modern world, they are perfect places to chat, cry or laugh with family and friends.

Thanks, of course, to my loving family, exceptional friends and my two hero boys, who make getting up the following day, with a hangover, worthwhile.

Special thanks to my friend of nearly twenty years, who was the first person to back me to continue this dream.

HOW TO GET INVOLVED

Since publishing my first book of pub crawls in autumn 2023, I have launched Historic Pub Crawls across social media, using the handle @historicpubcrawls, and begun to revisit all the pubs featured in my books.

It is great to meet and spend time with the landlords and staff, rediscover some of the areas, continually improve the details in these books and sample exciting new beers.

The best part about sharing the journey on social media has been receiving suggestions for new routes and pubs to explore.

If you are not already following me then please do, and join in, on the platforms below, as I love to hear about pubs I've missed or should be going to next as we explore more of the country – and the world – in the future.

Find me on TikTok, Instagram and YouTube: @historicpubcrawls.

ABOUT THE AUTHOR

Thomas has been running a pub crawl for his birthday almost every year since his mid-twenties.

After years working in technology, and following the closure of his startup, he decided to compile the years of fun into a handy guide that could be shared with others.

With his debut self-published book in hand, he walked into the first pub and asked for a free pint to film for his social media accounts, before a quick rejection left him slinking off without footage or a pint.

Fast-forward twelve months, and with over 250,000 followers, regular slots on national and local radio, and appearances on ITV and the BBC, he is a passionate champion of the community spirit that pubs bring to the heart of towns and cities across the UK.

When he is not writing or in the pub, he plays guitar and piano, and likes tattoos, crazy trousers and yellow shoes.

He lives in north-west London with his two sons.

NOTES